JOURNEY WITHOUT GOAL

DHARMA OCEAN SERIES

JOURNEY WITHOUT GOAL

The Tantric Wisdom of the Buddha

Chögyam Trungpa

PRAJÑĀ PRESS ● BOULDER & LONDON ● 1981

Prajñā Press
Great Eastern Book Company
P.O. Box 271
Boulder, Colorado 80306

Printed in the United States of America

"Lord Marpa's Praise to the Gurus" is excerpted from *The Biography of Marpa the Translator*, translated by the Nālandā Translation Committee under the direction of Chögyam Trungpa, to be published by Shambhala Publications, Inc.

This book is published in the Dharma Ocean Series. It is based on a series of lectures delivered by Chögyam Trungpa in the Buddhist Studies Department of Naropa Institute, Summer 1974.

LIBRARY OF CONGRESS CATALOGING IN PUBLICATION DATA
Trungpa, Chogyam, 1939—
    Journey without goal.

    (Dharma ocean series)
    Includes index.
    1. Tantric Buddhism—Doctrines—Addresses, essays, lectures. 2. Spiritual life (Tantric Buddhism)—Addresses, essays, lectures. I. Title. II. Series.
BQ8918.7.T78   294.3'925   81-13894
ISBN O-87773-755-X (pbk.)   AACR2

AN IMPRINT OF SHAMBHALA PUBLICATIONS, INC.

CONTENTS

ILLUSTRATIONS

Frontispiece. *Padma Trime, Jamgön Kongtrül of Sechen* (1901?– 1960). The root guru of·Chögyam Trungpa and an incarnation of Lodrö Thaye, Jamgön Kongtrül I.

Page 18.   *Lodrö Thaye, Jamgön Kongtrül I* (1813–1899). Often referred to as Jamgön Kongtrül the Great, Lodrö Thaye was a leader of the Rime movement (see Chapter 10). This painting is from the lineage thangkas at Rumtek Monastery in Sikkim, India. Photo used by the gracious permission of His Holiness the Sixteenth Gyalwa Karmapa, Rangjung Rikpe Dorje.

Page 30.   *The Mandala of Kalacakra.* A two-dimensional representation of the mandalas of body, speech, and mind of the *Kalacakra Tantra*.

Page 46.   *Jetsün Milarepa* (1040–1123). The chief disciple of Marpa, Milarepa is renowned for his songs of devotion and realization. This statue was a shrine object of Gampopa, Milarepa's chief disciple. *Photo credit:* George Holmes and Blair Hansen.

Page 64.   *Cakrasamvara and Vajravarahi.* Two of the principal yidams, or "personal deities," of the Kagyü school of Tibetan Buddhism, used in tantric visualization practice. This statue was a shrine object of Naropa, Marpa's guru. *Photo credit:* George Holmes and Blair Hansen.

Page 76.   *Vajra and Ghanta (bell).* *Photo credit:* George Holmes.

Page 100.   *Vajradhara.* The dharmakaya buddha. A tantric manifestation of the Buddha, Vajradhara is depicted as dark blue. Painting by Sherapalden Beru. *Photo credit:* George Holmes and Blair Hansen.

Page 124.   *Evam.* The personal seal of Chögyam Trungpa and the Trungpa tülkus (see Chapter 14). *Design:* Molly K. Nudell.

Page 132.   *Rangjung Dorje, Karmapa III* (1284–1339). A great vajrayana scholar and teacher, famous for bringing together the teachings of ati yoga with anuttara tantra. This painting is from the lineage thangkas at Rumtek Monastery in Sikkim, India. Photo used by the gracious permission of His Holiness the Sixteenth Gyalwa Karmapa, Rangjung Rikpe Dorje.

ACKNOWLEDGMENTS

Journey without Goal is based on a series of fifteen lectures presented by Vajracarya the Venerable Chögyam Trungpa, Rinpoche, at Naropa Institute during the summer of 1974. Under his guidance, Mrs. Judith Lief, then the Editor-in-Chief at Vajradhatu, began editing the lectures for publication in 1975. Working with the author and other members of the editorial department, she completed the major part of the manuscript before leaving to become the Dean of Naropa Institute in 1980.

The preparation of the final draft of the manuscript has been a collaborative effort by members of the editorial department: Mrs. Sarah Levy, Mrs. Barbara Blouin, Mrs. Helen Berliner, and myself. We have tried to maintain Mrs. Lief's approach to the material, which always respected the language of the original and showed an acute sensitivity to meaning and tone.

We are deeply indebted to the Vajracarya for the original presentation of this material and for allowing us the opportunity to deepen our own understanding through working with him on the manuscript.

We would like to thank the Nālandā Translation Committee for the translation from the Tibetan of the two poems that appear in the book. The first, "Intensifying Devotion in One's Heart" is by Jamgön Kongtrül the Great, whose contributions to the Practice Lineage of Tibetan Buddhism are discussed in Chapter Ten, "Abhisheka." The second, "Lord Marpa's

Praise to the Gurus," is by Marpa the Translator, the first Tibetan holder of the Kagyü lineage. It is taken from a larger work in progress, *The Life of Marpa*, to be published by Shambhala Publications. Particular thanks go to Miss Christine Keyser of the translation committee, who completed the initial draft of the translation of Jamgön Kongtrül's poem; and to Mr. Larry Mermelstein, the executive director of the committee, for editorial contributions to the entire manuscript.

We would also like to express our thanks to the Vajra Regent Ösel Tendzin and to Dr. Reginald Ray, Chairman of the Buddhist Studies Department at Naropa Institute, for their careful reading of the final typescript. As well, we would like to acknowledge the efforts of the many volunteers—typists, transcribers, and others—who worked on this book. Finally, we would like to thank the publisher, Mr. Samuel Bercholz, and the staff of Prajñā Press for their support of this book.

The reader may note that the language in this book is often poetic and evocative. These qualities have been treated as essential rather than incidental aspects of the original lectures, since they express most vividly the awake and brilliant experience of the vajra world.

The vajrayana wisdom that is presented here is powerful and authentic. We hope that this book will lead to a greater appreciation and understanding of tantric Buddhism, and we share in the author's wish that this book may benefit sentient beings and bring them to the path of dharma.

Carolyn Rose Gimian
Vajradhatu Editorial Department

Introduction

The teachings of the Buddha are a treasury of wisdom that has been passed down from teacher to student for over 2,500 years. Many styles of teaching have developed, but all of the schools of Buddhism present the means to realize the awakened state of mind, and all of them emulate the example of the Buddha, the Awakened One. This is a very important point to realize, particularly in the context of this book, which presents tantra, or the vajrayana teachings of Buddhism. Many people in America have heard about tantra as the "sudden path"—the quick way to enlightenment. Or they may have heard that tantra is a form of free expression or sexual liberation or some kind of full-blown emotionalism. But it is important to realize that tantra is not separate from the rest of the Buddhist path. Exotic ideas about tantra are not just misconceptions; they could be quite destructive. It is both dangerous and fruitless to attempt to practice tantra without first establishing a firm ground in the basic Buddhist teachings.

The Buddhist path is traditionally divided into three major yanas or vehicles: the hinayana, the mahayana, and the vajrayana. *Hinayana* literally means the "small or lesser vehicle," but it would

1

be more accurate to call it the "narrow way." The hinayana is small or narrow in the sense that the strict discipline of meditation narrows down, or tames, the speed and confusion of mind, allowing the mind to rest in its own place. The hinayana is also called the "immediate yana" because hinayana practice allows simple and direct experience of our own minds and of the world. We begin to realize that whatever we experience—whether good or bad, positive or negative—is workable, tamable.

As well as the discipline of meditation, the hinayana also stresses the importance of postmeditation discipline. Discipline in Sanskrit is *shila*, and in Tibetan it is *tsültrim (tshul-khrims)*. *Tsül* means "proper" or "appropriate"; *trim* means "regulation," "law," or "norm." So *tsültrim* is practicing "proper conduct" or "proper discipline," according to the example of the Buddha.

During his lifetime, the Buddha established disciplinary rules of conduct that are strictly applied in monastic life. These are called the *vinaya* in Sanskrit, or *dülwa ('dul-ba)* in Tibetan. Both *vinaya* and *dülwa* literally mean "taming." So in general, vinaya can be understood as any discipline that we practice in order to tame our being.

In the hinayana, the only way to conduct ourselves is according to the message of vinaya, the message of discipline. Through practicing the proper conduct of tsültrim, our body, speech, and mind are thoroughly tamed, and we are able to quell, or cool off, the heat of neurosis. Because of that, we are able to practice the greater hinayana discipline of not causing harm to ourselves and others. And finally, based on practicing such total discipline, we are able to achieve what is called "individual liberation" (Skt. *pratimoksha*, Tib. *so-sor-tharpa*). Individual liberation is a tremendous accomplishment, which enables us to express our basic goodness as human beings.

The *mahayana*, or the "great vehicle," is like a wide, open highway in contrast to the narrow path of hinayana discipline. The mahayana goes beyond the hinayana ideal of individual liberation alone. Its aim is the liberation of all sentient beings, which means that everyone, everything, is included in the vast vision of mahayana. All the chaos and confusion and suffering of ourselves and others is part of the path.

The primary discipline of the mahayana is helping others, putting others before ourselves. The training of the mahayana practitioner is to exchange himself for others. As a well-known mahayana slogan puts it: "Gain and victory to others; loss and defeat to oneself." However, it should be clear that this attitude is not based on self-denial or martyrdom, but rather springs from the development of genuine warmth and compassion. Thus, the mahayana is expansive and embracing.

The third yana, the *vajrayana*, literally means the "diamond or indestructible vehicle." The idea of indestructibility here is the discovery of indestructible wakefulness, the discovery of our own innate awakened state of mind, or vajra nature. Since this book deals with the vajrayana teachings, it seems unnecessary to explain too much about them here. However, it is extremely important to understand at the outset that the vajrayana is a continuation of the previous two yanas and that without proper training in the hinayana and mahayana disciplines, it is impossible to step onto the tantric path.

Tantra literally means "continuity" or "thread." Hinayana, mahayana, and vajrayana are a continuous thread of sympathy and sanity, which is never broken. Vajrayana is further and greater expansion. It is the expression of greater sanity and greater sympathy, arising from the practice of hinayana and mahayana.

Throughout this book the reader will find numerous warnings about the dangers of vajrayana and the importance of beginning at the beginning—with the practice of meditation. When I presented this material at Naropa Institute in the summer of 1974, I felt that it was my duty to warn people about the dangers of vajrayana and also to proclaim the sacredness of these teachings—which go hand in hand.

The audience was a very interesting mixture. There were many people who we might call "spiritual shoppers," people sampling tantra as one more interesting spiritual "trip." There were also a number of people who were quite innocent and open. They happened onto this class by various coincidences and had very little idea of what tantra, or spirituality at all, might be. As well, there were a number of committed students who had been practicing meditation for some time. It was quite a challenge to present tantra to such a mixed group. But for all of these people, it was necessary to stress again and again the importance of meditation as the foundation of all Buddhist practice and the danger of ignoring this prescription.

The entire Buddhist path is based on the discovery of egolessness and the maturing of insight or knowledge that comes from egolessness. In the hinayana, we discover the nonexistence of self through the practice of meditation. Assuming a dignified sitting posture, identifying with the breath, and simply noting thoughts and feelings— basic discursiveness—we begin to make friends with ourselves in a fundamental sense.

By applying mindfulness, or bare attention, to whatever arises during meditation, we begin to see that there is no permanence or solidity to our thought process, and at some point, we begin to realize that there is no permanence or solidity to us. In Sanskrit, the meditative practice of mindfulness is called *shamatha* and in Tibetan it is *shiné (zhi-gnas)*. *Shiné* literally means the development of "peace." The meaning of peace here is precisely this sense of taming the wildness of mind so that we are alert and able to experience ourselves directly. We are not talking about peace as some kind of trance state: shamatha is the first step in waking up.

Mindfulness naturally leads to the development of awareness, which is a sense of expansion, being aware of the environment or space in which we are being mindful. Awareness brings tremendous interest in things, people, and the world altogether. We begin to develop sympathy and caring for others. The practice of awareness in Sanskrit is called *vipashyana* and in Tibetan, *lhagthong (lhag-mthong)*, which literally means "clear seeing." Vipashyana is traditionally connected both with the practice of meditation and with the formal study of the teachings and postmeditation activities in general. Vipashyana provides a link between the insight that is developed in meditation practice and our everyday experience. It allows us to carry that meditative insight or awareness into our daily lives.

Through the insight that comes from vipashyana, we begin to make a further discovery of egolessness. We begin to develop a precise understanding of how mind functions and how confusion is generated. We are able to see how the belief in ego causes tremendous pain and suffering to ourselves and others.

From this comes the desire to renounce samsara, the wheel of confused existence—the world of ego. Renunciation is expressed as the desire to refrain from harming ourselves and others. As well, we begin to long for the path that will liberate us from confusion. We begin to develop confidence in the Buddha as the enlightened example; in the dharma, or teachings of Buddhism, which are the path; and in the sangha, the community of practitioners who follow this path. Renunciation is utterly and absolutely necessary if we wish to practice the teachings of the Buddha. This theme runs through the entire path, from beginning to end. At the vajrayana level, renunciation is connected with devotion to the teacher, the vajra master. Devotion to the teacher in the vajrayana demands the total surrender of ego, the complete renunciation of all clinging to self.

Because of the discovery of egolessness in shamatha and the development of interest and sympathy in vipashyana, we naturally begin to expand our sense of warmth and friendliness to others. We are less interested in "this," "I," "me," and more interested in "that." The mahayana path is based on this discovery that others are more important than ourselves. Because we have discovered egolessness, because we have discovered that *me* does not exist, we find that there is lots of room, lots of space, in which to help others. That is the basis of compassion, *karuna*. Compassion in the Buddhist tradition is not based on guilt; it is based on having greater vision, because we can afford to do so.

The mahayana teachings are profound and vast, and what I am presenting here is like a drop in the ocean of the mahayana dharma. Nevertheless, helping others is absolutely essential. This is true, not only in mahayana practice, but in vajrayana as well. Trying to practice vajrayana without compassion is like swimming in molten lead—it is deadly. All of the power and the magic of vajrayana is based on working for the benefit of others and surrendering ourselves—absolutely.

The vajrayana teachings are very precious; they are very close to my heart and they are my inheritance, so I do not pass them on lightly. Still, I am delighted that we can present tantra in the American world. What is presented here is like a map; it is an entirely different experience to actually make the journey. It requires a guide to make this journey, and as well, we must make the proper preparations: our minds must be tamed and trained through the practice of meditation. Only then can we see the vajra world.

As I have said, presenting these talks originally was quite demanding, but it was equally worthwhile. For those who connected with what was being transmitted, the experience of hearing these lectures was one of discovering devotion and beginning to surrender ego. It is my hope that, in a similar fashion, this book will inspire others to step onto the path of dharma.

> Vajracarya the Venerable
> Chögyam Trungpa, Rinpoche
> 10 July 1981
> Boulder, Colorado

INTENSIFYING DEVOTION IN ONE'S HEART:

The Supplication "Crying to the Gurus from Afar"

by Jamgön Kongtrül Lodrö Thaye

NAMO GURAVE

This practice of crying to the gurus from afar is well known to everyone. The key to invoking blessings is devotion, which is aroused by sadness and renunciation. This is not a mere platitude, but is born in the center of one's heart and in the depths of one's bones. With decisive conviction that there is no other buddha who is greater than the guru, recite this melodic tune.

> Guru, think of me.
> Kind root guru, think of me.
>
> Essence of the buddhas of the three times,
> Source of the holy dharma—what has been told and what has
>   been experienced—
> Master of the sangha, the noble assembly,
> Root guru, think of me.
>
> Great treasure of blessings and compassion,
> Source of the two siddhis,
> Buddha activity that bestows whatever is desired,
> Root guru, think of me.

Guru Amitābha, think of me.
Look upon me from the realm of dharmakāya, simplicity.
Lead us of evil karma who wander in saṃsāra
To the pure land of great bliss.

Guru Avalokiteśvara, think of me.
Look upon me from the realm of sambhogakāya, luminosity.
Pacify completely the suffering of the six realms.
Shake us from the depths of the three realms of saṃsāra.

Guru Padmākara, think of me.
Look upon me from the lotus light of Cāmara.[1]
The wretched Tibetan people who are without refuge in this
    dark age,
Quickly protect with your compassion.

Guru Yeshe Tsogyal,[2] think of me.
Look upon me from the celestial realm, the city of great bliss.
Help us who commit evil deeds to cross the ocean of saṃsāra
To the great city of liberation.

Gurus of the kama and terma lineages,[3] think of me.
Look upon me from the wisdom realm of unity.
Break through the dark dungeon of my confused mind.
Make the sun of realization arise.

Omniscient Trime Öser,[4] think of me.
Look upon me from the realm of the five spontaneous wisdom
    lights.
Help me to strengthen my primordially pure mind
And master the four stages of ati yoga.[5]

Incomparable Lord Atīśa, father and son,[6] think of me.
Look upon me from amidst one hundred devas in Tuṣita.
Arouse in me bodhicitta,
The essence of emptiness and compassion.

Three supreme siddhas—Marpa, Mila, and Gampopa—think of
    me.
Look upon me from the vajra realm of great bliss.

May I attain the supreme siddhi of mahāmudrā, bliss and
  emptiness,
And awaken dharmakāya in my heart.

Karmapa, lord of the world, think of me.
Look upon me from the space which tames all beings everywhere.
Help me to realize that all dharmas are insubstantial and illusory.
Make appearance and mind dawn as the three kāyas.

Kagyüs of the four great and eight lesser lineages, think of me.
Look upon me from the land of sacred outlook.
Help me to clear away my confusion in the fourth moment
And perfect my experience and realization.

Five Sakya forefathers,[7] jetsüns, think of me.
Look upon me from the realm of inseparable saṃsāra and
  nirvāṇa.
Help me to unite the completely pure view, meditation, and
  action
And walk upon the supreme secret path.

Incomparable Shangpa Kagyü,[8] think of me.
Look upon me from the completely pure buddha land.
Help me to learn properly the practice that liberates through
  skillful means
And attain the unity of nonlearning.

Great siddha, Thangtong Gyalpo,[9] think of me.
Look upon me from the realm of effortless compassion.
Help me to practice the yogic action of realizing insubstantiality.
Help me to master prāṇa and mind.

Only father, Phadampa Sanggye,[10] think of me.
Look upon me from the realm of accomplishing the highest
  action.
May the blessings of your lineage enter my heart
And may auspicious coincidence arise in all directions.

Only mother, Machik Lapkyi Drönma, think of me.
Look upon me from the realm of prajñāpāramitā.
Help me to uproot ego-fixation, the cause of pride,
And realize the truth of egolessness beyond conception.

Omniscient enlightened one of Tölpo,[11] think of me.
Look upon me from the realm endowed with all the supreme
     aspects.
Help me to still the shifting breaths in the central channel
And attain the immovable vajra body.

Jetsün Tāranātha,[12] think of me.
Look upon me from the realm of the three mudrās.
May I tread the secret vajra path unhindered.
And attain the rainbow body in the celestial realm.

Jamyang Khyentse Wangpo,[13] think of me.
Look upon me from the wisdom realm of the two kinds of
     knowing.
Help me to remove the obscurations of my ignorance
And expand the vision of supreme knowledge.

Ösel Trülpe Dorje, think of me.
Look upon me from the realm of the five rainbow light rays.
Help me to cleanse the impurities of bindu, prāṇa, and mind
And attain enlightenment of this youthful kāya in the vase.[14]

Padma Do Ngak Lingpa, think of me.
Look upon me from the unchanging realm of bliss and emptiness.
Enable me to completely fulfill
All the intentions of the victorious ones and their sons.

Ngakwang Yönten Gyatso,[15] think of me.
Look upon me from the realm of the union of space and
     wisdom.
May the habit of solidifying reality fall apart
And may I bring whatever occurs to the path.

Son of the victorious ones, Lodrö Thaye, think of me.
Look upon me from your nature of maitrī and compassion.
Enable me to realize that all beings are my kind parents
And wholeheartedly accomplish the benefit of others.

Padma Kargyi Wangchuk, think of me.
Look upon me from the realm of great bliss and luminosity.
Help me to liberate the five poisons into the five wisdoms.
And destroy my clinging to loss and gain.

Tennyi Yungtrung Lingpa, think of me.
Look upon me from the realm in which saṃsāra and nirvāṇa are
   equal.
May natural devotion be born in my being.
May realization and liberation simultaneously increase.

Kind root guru, think of me.
Look upon me from the top of my head, the place of great bliss.
May I meet my own mind, the face of dharmakāya
And attain buddhahood in one lifetime.

Alas!
Sentient beings like myself, evildoers with bad karma,
Have wandered in saṃsāra from beginningless time.
Even now we experience endless suffering,
And yet not even an instant of remorse has occurred.
Guru, think of me; look upon me quickly with compassion.
Grant your blessings so that I give rise to renunciation from my
   depths.

Although I have obtained a free and well-favored human birth,
I have wasted it in vain.
I am constantly distracted by the activities of this futile life.
Unable to accomplish the great objective of liberation and over-
   come by laziness,
I return empty-handed from a land of jewels.
Guru, think of me; look upon me quickly with compassion.
Grant your blessings so that I fulfill the purpose of human
   birth.

There is no one on earth who will not die.
Even now, one after another they pass away.
I also will die very soon,
And yet like an idiot, I prepare to live for a long time.
Guru, think of me; look upon me quickly with compassion.
Grant your blessings so that I curtail my worthless schemes.

I will become separated from my lovers and friends.
The wealth and food which I hoarded in miserliness will be
   enjoyed by others.
Even this body I hold so dear will be left behind.

My consciousness will wander in the unknown pardos of saṃsāra.
Guru, think of me; look upon me quickly with compassion.
Grant your blessings so that I realize the futility of life.

The black darkness of fear escorts me along.
The fierce red wind of karma chases after me.
Yama's hideous messengers beat and hack me.
Thus, I experience the unbearable suffering of the lower realms.
Guru, think of me; look upon me quickly with compassion.
Grant your blessings so that I free myself from the chasms of
the lower realms.

My faults are as large as a mountain, but I conceal them within
me.
Others' faults are as minute as a sesame seed, but I proclaim
and condemn them.
I boast about my virtues, though I don't even have a few.
I call myself a dharma practitioner and practice only nondharma.
Guru, think of me; look upon me quickly with compassion.
Grant your blessings so that I subdue my selfishness and pride.

I hide the demon of ego-fixation within, which will ruin me
permanently.
All of my thoughts are the cause of perpetuating kleśas.
All of my actions have unvirtuous results.
I have not even gone toward the path of liberation.
Guru, think of me; look upon me quickly with compassion.
Grant your blessings so that I uproot my selfishness.

Just a little praise or blame makes me happy or sad.
A mere harsh word causes me to lose my armor of patience.
Even when I see helpless ones, compassion does not arise.
When needy people come to me, I am tied up by a knot of
miserliness.
Guru, think of me; look upon me quickly with compassion.
Grant your blessings so that my mind is mixed with the dharma.

I hold on dearly to futile saṃsāra.
For the sake of food and clothing, I completely abandon per-
manent objectives.

Though I have everything I need, I constantly want more and
　　more.
My mind is duped by insubstantial and illusory things.
Guru, think of me; look upon me quickly with compassion.
Grant your blessings so that I am not attached to this life.

I cannot endure even the slightest physical or mental pain,
Yet I am so stubborn that I have no fear of falling into the lower
　　realms.
Though I actually see unerring cause and effect,
Still I do not act virtuously, but perpetuate evil.
Guru, think of me; look upon me quickly with compassion.
Grant your blessings so that conviction in karma arises in me.

I am hateful toward enemies and attached to friends.
I am stupified in darkness as to what should be accepted and
　　rejected.
When practicing the dharma, I fall under the influence of
　　discursiveness, sloth, and sleep.
When acting against the dharma, I am clever and my senses are
　　alert.
Guru, think of me; look upon me quickly with compassion.
Grant your blessings so that I conquer my enemy, the kleśas.

My outer appearance is that of an authentic dharma practitioner,
But inside, my mind is not mixed with the dharma.
Like a poisonous snake, the kleśas are concealed within me.
When I encounter bad circumstances, my hidden faults as a bad
　·practitioner are revealed.
Guru, think of me; look upon me quickly with compassion.
Grant your blessings so that I can tame my own mind.

I don't realize my own bad faults.
I maintain the form of a practitioner while engaging in various
　　nondharmic pursuits.
Because of the kleśas, I am naturally accustomed to unvirtuous
　　actions.
Again and again I give birth to a mind of virtue, but again and
　　again it falls apart.
Guru, think of me; look upon me quickly with compassion.
Grant your blessings so that I see my own faults.

As each day passes, my death is nearer and nearer.
As each day passes, my being is harsher and harsher.
Though I attend my guru, my devotion becomes gradually
obscured.
Love, affection, and sacred outlook toward my dharma compan-
ions grow smaller and smaller.
Guru, think of me; look upon me quickly with compassion.
Grant your blessings so that I tame my stubborn nature.

I've taken refuge, aroused bodhicitta, and made supplications,
But devotion and compassion are not born in the depths of my
heart.
I give lip service to dharmic action and spiritual practice,
But they become routine and I'm not touched by them.
Guru, think of me; look upon me quickly with compassion.
Grant your blessings so that I may be one with the dharma.

All suffering comes from desiring happiness for oneself.
Although it is said that buddhahood is attained by considering
the welfare of others,
I arouse supreme bodhicitta but secretly cherish selfishness.
Not only do I not benefit others, I casually cause them harm.
Guru, think of me; look upon me quickly with compassion.
Grant your blessings so that I exchange myself for others.

The guru is buddha in person, but I regard him as an ordinary
man.
I forget his kindness in giving profound instructions.
When he doesn't do what I want, I lose heart.
His actions and behavior are clouded over by my doubts and
disbelief.
Guru, think of me; look upon me quickly with compassion.
Grant your blessings so that unobscured devotion will increase.

My own mind is the Buddha, but I never realize this.
Discursive thoughts are dharmakāya, but I don't realize this.
This is the unfabricated, innate state, but I cannot keep to this.
Naturalness is things as they really are, but I have no conviction
in this.
Guru, think of me; look upon me quickly with compassion.
Grant your blessings so that my mind will be spontaneously
liberated.

Death is certain to come, but I am unable to take this to heart.
The holy dharma truly benefits, but I am unable to practice it properly.
Karma and its result are certainly true, but I do not properly discriminate what to accept or reject.
Mindfulness and awareness are certainly necessary, but not stabilizing them, I am swept away by distractions.
Guru, think of me; look upon me quickly with compassion.
Grant your blessings so that I maintain undistracted mindfulness.

Because of my former evil actions, I was born at the end of the dark age.
All that I have previously done has caused me suffering.
Because of evil friends, I am darkened by the shadow of evil deeds.
My dharma practice has been sidetracked by my meaningless chatter.
Guru, think of me; look upon me quickly with compassion.
Grant your blessings so that I completely accomplish the holy dharma.

Grant your blessings so that I give birth to deep sadness.
Grant your blessings so that my worthless schemes are curtailed.
Grant your blessings so that I take to heart the certainty of death.
Grant your blessings so that conviction in karma arises in me.
Grant your blessings so that the path is free from obstacles.
Grant your blessings so that I am able to exert myself in practice.
Grant your blessings so that unfortunate circumstances are brought to the path.
Grant your blessings so that I continually apply my antidotes.
Grant your blessings so that genuine devotion arises in me.
Grant your blessings so that I glimpse the natural state.
Grant your blessings so that insight is awakened in my heart.
Grant your blessings so that I uproot confusion.
Grant your blessings so that I attain buddhahood in one lifetime.

Precious guru, I supplicate you.
Kind lord of the dharma, I cry to you with longing.

I am an unworthy person who relies on no one but you.
Grant your blessings so that my mind mixes inseparably with
yours.

I was first requested by some devoted monks to compose a supplication, but I was delayed in fulfilling their request. Recently, Samdrup
Drönma, a lady practitioner of noble family, and Deva Rakṣita
earnestly urged me. Therefore, I, Lodrö Thaye, who merely hold
the appearance of a guru in this dark age, wrote this at the great
meditation center, Dzongshö Deshek Düpa.[16] May virtue increase.

Translated by the Nālandā Translation Committee.

NOTES

1. Cāmara is one of the two islands next to the southern continent of Jambudvīpa.
On this island, Padmākara (Padmasambhava) is said to now reside in a palace on the
Copper Colored Mountain.

2. Yeshe Tsogyal is one of the two chief consorts of Padmākara (Padmasambhava),
the other being Mandaravā. She is the author of a biography of Padmasambhava
(*Padma thang yig*).

3. The kama lineage is the unbroken oral tradition that has been passed down from
Vajradhara Buddha to one's present root guru. The terma lineage consists of sacred
objects and teachings that were hidden by Padmākara and other teachers until the
time was right for their unveiling. Then, they would be discovered and promul-
gated by teachers known as tertöns ("terma discoverers").

4. This is the name that was conferred on the famous Nyingma teacher, Longchen
Rabjam (1308–1364), by Padmākara in a vision.

5. These four stages (snang bzhi) are: revelation of dharmatā, increasing experience, maturation of insight, and exhausting dharmatā.

6. Atīśa's (982–1054) spiritual son here is Dromtön (1004–1063), his main Tibetan
disciple and the founder of the Kadampa school.

7. These are five great and early teachers in the Sakya lineage. They are Künga
Nyingpo (1092–1158), Sönam Tsemo (1142–1182), Trakpa Gyaltsen (1147–1216),
Sakya Paṇḍita (1182–1231), and Phakpa (1235–1280).

8. The Shangpa Kagyü is a sect of the Kagyü lineage founded by Barapa Gyaltsen
Palzang (1310–1391). However, it traces its origin back to Shang Khyungpo Naljorpa

(990–1139?), a follower of Pön who converted to Buddhism. He had many Indian gurus, one of them being Niguma, Nāropa's wife and disciple.

9. Thangtong Gyalpo (1385–1464) is famed throughout Tibet as a great siddha and builder of iron bridges.

10. Phadampa Sanggye (died 1117) is a South Indian teacher who brought the practices of shije (pacifying) and chö (cutting) to Tibet. His main disciple and consort was the Tibetan woman, Machik Lapkyi Drönma (1055–1149) who spread the lineage of the chö teachings in Tibet.

11. Tölpopa Sherap Gyaltsen (1292–1361) is the founder of the Jonangpa school which mainly emphasized the *Kālacakra-tantra* and the teaching of tathāgatagarbha. The shen tong (gzhan stong, empty of other) view of mādhyamika that the Jonangpa evolved was quite controversial among the mainstream adherents of the rang tong (rang stong, empty of self) view; however, this shen tong view was a powerful principle for the Rime thought in general and in particular for Jamgön Kongtrül.

12. Tāranātha (born 1575) is one of the most famous teachers of the Jonangpa school, having written a well-known history of Buddhism in India as well as several important texts on the *Kālacakra*.

13. Jamyang Khyentse Wangpo (1820–1892) is one of the leaders of the nineteenth-century Rime movement in Tibet. He was the root guru of Jamgön Kougtrül Lodrö Thaye. Ösel Trülpe Dorje and Padma Do Njak Lingpa are the names given to him from a prophecy of Thangtong Gyalpo (see following two stanzas).

14. This image is used in ati teachings to describe the nature of primordial enlightenment. The youthful kāya is enlightenment which is always present. The vase contains all dharmas and gives rise to all phenomena.

15. The next four names all belong to the author of this text, Jamgön Kongtrül Lodrö Thaye. The first name he received when he took the vinaya vows, the second when he took the bodhisattva vow, and the third when he received abhiṣeka—formally becoming a student of the vajrayāna. The last name was given to him when he was formally recognized as a tertön, a discoverer of terma.

   The reason Jamgön Kongtrül includes himself in the guru supplication is that he composed this text for his disciples' practice at their request.

16. This meditation center is northeast of Shigatse, located at Zambulung in upper Shang. Jamyang Khyentse Wangpo also resided here at one time and had an important vision of the eight manifestations of Padmākara.

CHAPTER ONE

The Tantric Practitioner

The tantric teachings of Buddhism are extremely sacred and, in some sense, inaccessible. Tantric practitioners of the past have put tremendous energy and effort into the study of tantra. Now we are bringing tantra to North America, which is a landmark in the history of Buddhism. So we can not afford to make our own studies into supermarket merchandise.

A tantric revolution took place in India many centuries ago. The wisdom of that tradition has been handed down orally from generation to generation by the great mahasiddhas, or tantric masters. Therefore, tantra is known as the ear-whispered, or secret, lineage. However, the notion of secrecy does not imply that tantra is like a foreign language. It is not as though our parents speak two languages, but they only teach us English so that they can use Chinese or Yiddish when they want to keep a secret from us. Rather, tantra introduces us to the actuality of the phenomenal world. It is one of the most advanced, sharp, and extraordinary perceptions that has ever developed. It is unusual and eccentric; it is powerful, magical, and outrageous; but it is also extremely simple.

In order to understand the phenomenon of tantra, or tantric

19

consciousness, we should be quite clear that we are not talking about tantra as a vague spiritual process. Tantra, or *vajrayana* Buddhism, is extremely precise, and it is unique. We can not afford to jumble the vajrayana into a spiritual or philosophical stew. Instead, we should discuss tantra technically, spiritually and personally—in a very exact sense—and we should discuss what the uniqueness of the tantric tradition has to offer to sentient beings.

In this book we will examine tantra theoretically. We are viewing the area that we might arrive at, at some point in the future. So it is a somewhat hypothetical situation, but at the same time we still could develop an experiential connection with it. The future of Buddhism depends on continuing to discover what the Buddha experienced and on sharing such experience with others. So there is a need to identify ourselves personally with tantric experience, rather than regarding tantra as one more spiritual trip.

Fundamentally, the vajrayana comes out of a complete understanding and comprehension of both *hinayana* and *mahayana* Buddhism. The development of the three yanas—hinayana, mahayana, and vajrayana—is one continuous process. In fact, the word *tantra*, or *gyü(rgyud)* in Tibetan, means "continuity." There is a continuous thread running through the Buddhist path, which is our personal experience and our commitment to the Buddhist teachings. Usually we think of a thread as starting somewhere. But according to the Buddhist teachings, the thread has no beginning, and therefore there is continuity. In fact, such a thread does not even exist, but at the same time, it is continuous.

At this point we are not yet in a position to discuss what tantra is. Since the continuity of tantra is based on personal experience, we first need to understand the person who is having the experience. That is, we need to know who is studying tantra: who is it, or what is it? So, to begin with, we have to go back to the beginning, and find out who is perceiving tantra, that is, who is the *tantrika* or tantric practitioner.

We could say that some people are tantric by nature. They are inspired in their lives; they realize that some reality is taking place in the true sense, and they feel that the experience of energy is relevant to them. They may feel threatened by energy or they may feel a lack of energy, but they have a personal interest in the world: the visual world, the auditory world, the world of the senses altogether. They are interested in how things work and how things are perceived. That sense of enormous interest, that interest in perceptions, is tantric by nature. However, one problem with inspired, future tantric practitioners is that they are often *too* fascinated by the world of the senses. There is something lacking: although they are inspired, they may not have made a genuine connection to the world of the senses, which presents problems in understanding true tantra. Still, they could be regarded as tantric fetuses, or potential members of the tantric family.

When we begin to explore who the tantric practitioner actually is, our inquiry takes us further and further back, right to the basis of Buddhist practice, which is the hinayana teachings. From this point of view, hinayana *is* tantra. One of the inspiring glimpses or experiences of the hinayana practitioner is the absence of self, which is also the absence of God. When we realize that there is no individual being or personality who is perceiving external entities, the situation becomes open. We don't have to limit things by having a conceptualized divine being, traditionally known as God. We are simply examining who we are. In examining who we are, we find, according to both the hinayana and the tantric observation, that we are nobody—rather, nonbody. We might ask, "How is that possible? I have a name. I have a body. I eat. I sleep. I lead my life. I wear clothes." But that is precisely the point: we misunderstand ourselves, our nonexistent selves. Because we eat, we sleep, we live and we have a name, we presume that something must be there. That common misunderstanding took place a long time ago, and it still takes place constantly, every single moment. Just because we have a name doesn't mean we have a self. How do we realize that? Because if we do not use such reference points as our name or our clothing, if we stop saying, "I eat, I sleep, I do such and such," then there is a big gap.

In a similar fashion, we often use reference points to show that we do not exist. We say we do *not* exist because of something else. We might say, "I do not exist because I am penniless." There is something wrong with that logic, because we still have a penny to be less of. However, this does not mean that we should try to destroy relative reference points. As an extreme example, during the 1960s some people made hysterical attempts not to exist. By destroying references and credentials such as draft cards and birth certificates, they hoped to become invisible. But creating their draft-card-less-ness was still a statement of deliberate individuality, and it was still fighting over the question of existence by struggling not to exist.

In the Buddhist tradition, discovering nonexistence, or egoless-ness, has nothing to do with destroying relative reference points. Whether we try to maintain such reference points or destroy them, we still have the same problem. The Buddhist approach is not to use any reference points at all—none whatsoever. Then we are not finding out whether we exist or not, but we are simply looking at ourselves directly, without any reference points—without even look-ing, we could say. That may be very demanding, but let it be so. Let us get to the heart of the matter.

When we attempt to see ourselves without reference points, we may find ourselves in a situation of not knowing what to do. We may feel completely lost, and we may think that what we are trying to do is very strange indeed: "I can't even begin. How can I do anything?" Then we might have an inkling of beginning at the beginning. Having to relate with the bewilderment of not knowing how to deal with ourselves without using reference points is getting closer to the truth. At the same time, we have not found the root of reality, if there is one at all.

We cannot find the beginning of the tantric thread unless we come to the conclusion that we do not exist. We might try to work out our nonexistence logically. However, the conclusion that we do not exist has to be experiential, and it also has to be beyond our stupidity and confusion. Our confusion at this point is not knowing how to begin. From that, we can start to feel the beginninglessness of the thread, and its endlessness as well. So we are getting some-where, but we still might feel rather stupid, like jellyfish or robots. There is no sense of discovery at all, and the whole thing seems rather flat.

According to the tantric tradition, the only way to find our way out of that confusion, or our way in, is by having a sense of humor about our predicament. We are trying to find ourselves, but we are not able to do so, and we feel enormously flat and heavy and in the way. Something is being a nuisance, but we cannot put our finger on exactly what it is. Nevertheless, something, somewhere, is being a nuisance. Or is it? If we view this with humor, we begin to find that even the flatness, the lack of inspiration, the solidity, and the confusion are dancing constantly. We need to develop a sense of excitement and dance rather than just trying to feel better. When we begin to dance with our humor, our apparent stupidity becomes somewhat uplifted. However, we do not know for sure whether we are just looking at ourselves humorously while our stupidity grows heavier all the time, or whether we might actually be able to cure ourselves. There is still something that is uncertain, completely confused, and very ambiguous.

At that point, we finally could start to relate with the ambiguity. In the tantric tradition, discovering that ambiguity is called "discovering the seed syllable." Ambiguity is called a "seed syllable" when it becomes a starting point rather than a source of problems. When we accept uncertainty as the working base, then we begin to discover that we do not exist. We can experience and appreciate the ambiguity as the source of confusion as well as the source of humor. The discovery of nonexistence comes from experiencing both the energy of humor and the heavy "thingness" or form of confusion. But form or thingness does not prove the existence of energy, and energy does not prove the existence of form. So there is no confirmation, just ambiguity. Therefore, we still find ourselves at a loss. However, at this point that feeling of being lost has the quality of freedom rather than the quality of confusion.

This experience of ambiguity is a personal experience rather than an analytical experience. We begin to realize that actually we do not exist. We do not exist because of our existence: that is the punchline of our ambiguity. And the world exists because of our nonexistence. We do not exist; therefore the world exists. There is an enormous joke behind the whole thing, a big joke. We might ask, "Who is playing such a joke on us?" It is difficult to say. We do not know who it is at all. We are so uncertain that we might not even have a question mark to put at the end of our sentence. Neverthe-less, that is our purpose in studying tantra: to find out who is the questioner, who set this question up altogether, if anyone at all.

The beginner's point of view is to realize nonexistence, to understand nonexistence, and to experience nonexistence. It is very important for us to realize that sight, smell, colors, emotions, formlessness, and form are all expressions of no-beginning, nonex-istence, egolessness. Such nonexistence has to be experienced per-sonally rather than analytically or philosophically. That personal experience is extremely important. In order for us to get into tantra properly, in order to become good tantra students, we have to go through the experience of nonexistence, however frustrating, con-fusing, or irritating it may seem. Otherwise, what we are doing is completely fruitless.

CHAPTER TWO

Vajra Nature

The vajrayana seems to have been widely misunderstood in the West. People have projected a lot of ideas onto it, believing it to be an expression of wildness and freedom. However, the cultivation of vajrayana has to be based on a very subtle, definite, ordinary, and real foundation. Otherwise, we are lost. Not only are we lost, but we are destroying ourselves.

In talking about the tantric tradition, we are not talking about playing with sex or aggression or colors or the phenomenal world. At this point we are simply developing a basic understanding of how tantra works. We have to be very conservative. We have to be very, very concerned with the fundamentals. I could say: "Don't worry. If you worry, that's your problem. If you don't worry, everything is going to be okay. Let's dance together. Let's play music together. Let's drink milk and honey." But that does not work, not at all. Talking about tantra is not such an easy matter.

Working with the energy of vajrayana is like dealing with a live electric wire. We can use switches, gloves, and all sorts of buffers in handling this live wire, but we also have the choice of using our bare hands and touching the live wire directly—in which case we are in trouble. The institution of tantra, not only Buddhist tantra but Hindu tantra as well, has been presented very generously to American students by many competent and great teachers. Still, many students get into trouble. They can't take it. They simply can't take it. They end up destroying themselves. They end up playing with the energy until it becomes a spiritual atomic bomb.

We might feel that working with tantra is like planting a little seed: we nourish it, make it germinate and send out shoots of greenery, and finally it will blossom as a beautiful flower. That is wishful thinking. We cannot approach tantra in that way. Instead, we have to realize that taking care of such a plant is not ordinary gardening. An extraordinary process is needed. Dealing with our state of being, our state of mind, is extraordinary in many ways. Moreover, dealing with our state of mind from the subtle tantric point of view is extremely dangerous—highly dangerous and equally highly productive. Therefore we should be very careful and open when we talk about vajrayana. Nonexistence is the only preparation for tantra, and we should realize that there is no substitute.

The experience of nonexistence brings a sense of delightful humor and, at the same time, complete openness and freedom. In addition, it brings an experience of complete indestructibility that is unchallengeable, immovable, and completely solid. The experience of indestructibility can only occur when we realize that nonexistence is possible, in the sense of being without reference points, without philosophical definitions, without even the notion of nonexistence.

The development of indestructibility or immovability is extremely important to understand. Such indestructibility can only come out of the state of nothingness, egolessness, or nonexistence. According to the Buddha, tantra is greater liberation, greater discipline, and greater vision. But this greater liberation is based on working with the potentialities and energies that exist within us. Therefore, without having some understanding of nonexistence, there is no point in discussing indestructibility.

When we consider someone to be indestructible, we generally mean that he is well established in his discipline, such as a person who has mastered the art of warfare or studied philosophy in great depth. Because such a person has mastered all sorts of techniques and training, we therefore consider him to be immovable or inde-structible. In fact, from the tantric point of view, the attempt to secure oneself with gadgetry is a source of vulnerability rather than indestructibility. In this case, we are not talking about indestructi-bility based on collecting information, tricks, or ideas. Instead we are referring to a basic attitude of trust in the nonexistence of our being.

In the tantric notion of indestructibility, there is no ground, no basic premise, and no particular philosophy except one's own expe-rience, which is extremely powerful and dynamic. It is a question of being rather than figuring out what to be, how to be. Usually we rely upon reference points, conceptual ideas, and feedback to give us guidelines as to how to be good or bad boys and girls, but such dependence is questionable. If you say to your doctor, "I have insomnia; how can I fall asleep?" the doctor responds by saying, "Take these pills. Then you will have no problem." In America in particular that approach has become a problem. In tantra, the point is not *how* to handle ourselves, but that we simply have to do it. We cannot trick ourselves into realizing the state of immovability, or indestructibility. Indestructibility is based on our experience, which is solid, dynamic, and unyielding.

In that way, tantric discipline does not cooperate with any deception at all; therefore it is regarded as indestructible, immov-able. The tantric approach of nonparticipation in the games that go on in the samsaric world, however, is something more than boycott-ing. When we boycott something, we do so in the name of a protest. We disagree with certain systems or certain ideas, and therefore we make a nuisance of ourselves. In this case, instead of boycotting the samsaric setup, we are fully and personally involved with it. We realize all the so-called "benefits" that the samsaric world might present to us—spiritual, psychological, and material goods of all kinds. We are fully aware of all the alternatives, but we do not yield to any of them at all. We are straightforward and hardheaded. That is the quality of immovability.

The word "hardheaded" is very interesting. When we say some-body is hardheaded, we mean that he is not taken in by anything. That is precisely what is meant by the term *vajra nature*: hardheadedness, vajra-headedness. Vajra is a quality of toughness and not being taken in by any kind of seduction. We also talk about "hard truth." Such truth is hard, unyielding, and uncomplimentary. When we receive news of someone's death, it is the hard truth. We cannot go back and say that it is not true. We cannot hire an attorney to argue the case or spend our money trying to bring the person back to life, because it is the hard truth. In the same way, vajra nature is hard truth. We cannot challenge or manipulate it in any way at all. It is both direct and precise.

The term *vajra* in Sanskrit or *dorje (rdo-rje)* in Tibetan means "having the qualities of a diamond." Like a diamond, vajra is tough and at the same time extremely precious. Unless we understand this basic vajra quality of tantra, or of the tantrika—this almost bull-headed quality of not yielding to any kind of seductions, to any little tricks or plays on words—we cannot understand vajrayana Buddhism at all.

Fundamentally speaking, indestructibility, or vajra nature, is basic sanity. It is the total experience of tantra, the experience of the enlightened state of being. This sanity is based on the experience of clarity, which comes from the practice of meditation. Through the meditation practice of the three yanas we discover a sense of clarity, unconditional clarity. Such clarity is ostentatious and has immense brilliance. It is very joyful and it has potentialities of everything. It is a real experience. Once we have experienced this brilliance, this farseeing, ostentatious, colorful, opulent quality of clarity, then there is no problem. That *is* vajra nature. It is indestructible. Because of its opulence and its richness, it radiates constantly, and immense, unconditional appreciation takes place. That combination of indestructibility and clarity is the basic premise of tantric Buddhist teachings.

We should understand how the vajrayana notion of brilliance differs from the notion of clear light as described in the *Tibetan Book of the Dead* and how it differs from the mahayana notion of luminosity. Clear light, according to the *Tibetan Book of the Dead*, is purely a phenomenological experience. You see whiteness as you die or as your consciousness begins to sink. Because the physical data of your body's habitual patterns are beginning to dissolve, you begin to enter another realm. You feel whitewashed, as if you were swimming in milk, or drowning in milk. You feel suffocated with whiteness, which is known as clear light. That is purely a phenomenological experience, not the true experience of clarity. On the other hand, the mahayana Buddhists talk about luminosity, called *prabhasvara* in Sanskrit, or *ösel (’od-gsal)* in Tibetan. Ösel means seeing things very precisely, clearly, logically, and skillfully. Everything is seen very directly; things are seen as they are. Nevertheless, neither prabhasvara nor the notion of clear light match the tantric notion of vajra clarity.

Vajrayana clarity has more humor. It also has more subtlety and dignity. Moreover, it is utterly, totally outrageous. Things are seen as they are, precisely; but at the same time things are also seeing us precisely. Because we are totally exposed and open and not afraid to be seen, a meeting point occurs. Something makes us realize that we cannot chicken out and say that our life is just a rehearsal. Something makes us realize that it is real. That state of being is not merely a phenomenological experience. It is a real state of being, a true state of being that is full and complete. That indestructibility and clarity are vajra nature, which is superior to any other approach to spirituality, even within the Buddhist tradition.

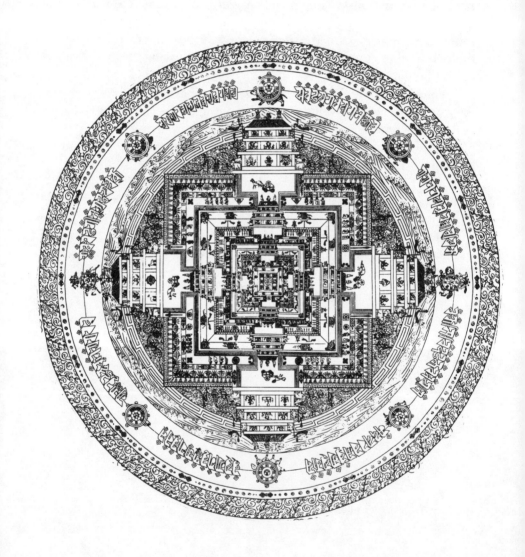

CHAPTER THREE

Mandala

There are three worlds presented in the tantric tradition: the world of perceptions, the world of the body, and the world of emotions. Our relationship with the world of perceptions is called the *outer mandala*; our relationship with the world of the body is called the *inner mandala*; and our relationship with the world of emotions is called the *secret mandala*.

OUTER MANDALA

We are constantly engaged in relationships with the ordinary world, that is, the world of *ayatanas* or the six sense perceptions: seeing, hearing, smelling, tasting, feeling, and thinking, the process which coordinates the other five. In Buddhism thinking is considered to be one of the senses. Our different perceptions are constantly being coordinated into a mandala. By *mandala* we mean interlocking relationships rather than an extraordinary magical circle. Mandala is simply the coordination of one point with another. For instance, in film-making the visual material is edited, and the sound has to be edited as well, so that the two work together.

31

The same thing happens in everyday life. When we enter a restaurant, we hear the clattering of pots and pans, and we begin to smell the food. At that point we may either get turned on or turned off by the restaurant's mandala. Or someone may introduce a friend to us: "This is a good friend of mine. I would like you to meet him." We say, "How are you?" and we sit down to talk with that person. That person speaks and behaves in a certain way, and we begin to feel that we like him, either on the grounds of our friend's recommendation or because we feel it is worthwhile to associate with such a person.

Perhaps our car is breaking down and we stop at a gas station. One of the passengers decides to step out and ask the attendant how far it is to the next motel. From the way that person behaves when he brings back the message, we can tell whether the answer is going to be favorable or disappointing. In that way, we always have a feeling about what is taking place.

According to tantra, that feeling, or intuitive setup, is a part of the external world. It is part of an actual relationship. Something is happening, or for that matter, something is not happening. Nevertheless, there is an actual relationship taking place constantly. Our experience of that relationship is not particularly based on superstition. We simply have a personal experience of the whole situation, a sense of the reality of mandala.

The outer mandala principle is the possibility of relating with a situation as a cohesive structure. Some setups are unpleasant, destructive, and unworkable; other setups are creative, workable, and pleasant. Mandalas are the general patterns, whether pleasant or unpleasant, that link us to the rest of the world, which is our world or our creation in any case.

When we begin to work with reality properly, an enormous relationship, a rapport, takes place between us and the external world. That rapport is taking place constantly, some kind of network or system of relations. It is as if something were circulating. For instance, when we are just about to catch the flu, we feel that the world is not particularly favorable to us. Whatever we experience and whatever we feel is somewhat strange. We feel that something is not quite clicking. We feel numb and unhealthy already. The world outside seems too solid, and we cannot relate that solidity to the softness or vulnerability in ourselves. The world seems hardened and heavy, and we cannot seem to make any connection with it. Those are the signs of a fever, an approaching flu. Although they seem to signal a discrepancy in our relationship with the world, that experience itself is an example of mandala principle.

According to the tantric tradition, the outer mandala principle is the external world and how we relate with it. However, the emphasis on relationship does not mean that the world is regarded as an intuitive or purely subjective world. It is simply the external world. For instance, the outer mandala is connected with how we relate with hot and cold. If we are outdoors in a hot climate and we walk into a highly air-conditioned building, we may get sick because we are not able to handle hot and cold properly. Our coordination with the world may not be quite right.

Usually, we experience such problems when we ignore the relationship between the world outside and our own world, our body. If we do not acknowledge our sense perceptions properly and thoroughly, we find ourselves in trouble—not because *what* we perceive is poisonous, but because *how* we perceive has become incompetent, haphazard, or confused, and therefore it has turned into poison. From that point of view, we cannot say that the phenomenal world we are living in—the traffic jams and the pollution and the inflation—is bad and devilish. We cannot condemn the world or put it into those kinds of conceptual packages. That approach does not work, because it means that we are fighting with our own phenomena.

Phenomena are ours: it is our country, our air, our earth, our food, our water, our electricity, our policemen. When we talk about the mandala setup we are speaking of an organic reality. We are not saying that we should reorganize the world, or that we should fight for it. We are talking about how we could look at it in an organic, natural way. The world could evolve *itself* according to our enlightenment—naturally. If you were a political activist, you might have difficulty in understanding this seemingly wishy-washy philosophy. You might say, "Don't we have to speak up? Don't we have to do something?" But when we talk about the tantric level of perception, we are not talking about concocting something. The outer mandala principle purely refers to actual, immediate relationships, visual, auditory, and conceptual relationships, with the so-called "world outside."

When we relate directly to the world, we can see that there is a thread of continuity. We can see the setup as a whole, rather than having only a partial view. According to the Buddhist path, there is nothing *other* than that whole world; therefore we could say that the tantric attitude toward reality is nontheistic. In the nontheistic approach to reality, the world is not divided between God and the Devil. The world is a totality in itself. It has its own muscles, its own brain, its own limbs, and its own circulation. The world has its own water system, electrical system, and sewage system automatically built in. They are already there. The problem we face is that we do not see that totality; we do not acknowledge it. We do not even get close to it, to see that it is actually true.

We are not talking about the totality of the world in the sense that everything should be good and perfect and fantastic, and nobody should acknowledge anything bad. We are talking about reality, in which good is made out of bad and bad is made out of good. Therefore, the world can exist in its own good/bad level, its self-existing level of dark and light, black and white, constantly. We are not fighting for either of those sides. Whatever there is, favorable or unfavorable, it is workable; it is the universe. That is why in the tantric tradition we talk about the world, or the cosmos, in terms of mandala.

Mandala is a totality; it has a universal quality. That totality is not a compromise, as if someone were to say, "If you tone down your badness and I tone down my goodness we will have a happy medium, with both good and bad toned down to a grey level." That kind of compromise is not a totality; it is just grey and depressing. In fact, that is one of the depressing aspects of some of the ecumenical movements taking place in this country and the rest of the world. They seem to be based on the feeling that everything should be okay and that everything is good. Badness should come up to the level of goodness, and goodness should come down to the level of badness, so that we can have some kind of happy medium. In that approach, there could be communist Buddhists or Nazi tantric practitioners. But somehow that does not work; it is too silly.

INNER MANDALA

We have been talking about the external world, or the world of perceptions, as a mandala that we are able to work with. The second type of world is the body, which is known as the inner mandala. This mandala is connected with how we handle our bodies in terms of our awareness, or sense of reality.

Developing awareness is quite deliberate. In the beginning we might feel that working deliberately with the body is too exaggerated a form of behavior. However, it seems to be necessary. We have never regarded our bodies as sacred property. The attitude of sacredness has been neglected, particularly in the Western world. Instead, life is regarded as a hassle. We were born, breast-fed or bottle-fed, and put into diapers. Those were our unpleasant facts of life. Now we can go to the toilet and drink our cup of tea—how victorious we are! We view it as a victory that we have survived all that. But we have not actually developed any art in our lives. We do not know how to care for our bodies.

Taking care of ourselves is regarded as an enormous hassle: getting up at a certain time, writing checks, going to the bank, going to a restaurant are all done humorlessly. Perhaps our only delight is to get drunk at a party. We have a fantastic time dancing with our partner, whoever it may be, and then we peacefully pass out. That is a very crude way of handling our bodies. There is no dignity in that, none whatsoever.

We may have been taught sophisticated table manners by our aristocratic parents. They may have taught us how to drink, how to use forks and knives, and how to sit properly and make good conversation. Still, there is some fundamental crudeness involved, because we have been taught a facade, rather than what should be felt. We could be extremely well mannered and able to pass through diplomatic circles immaculately and impeccably. Nevertheless, there could still be a crudeness of fundamentally not knowing how to relate with our cup of tea, our plate, our table, or our chair.

There are enormous problems with thinking that we can only trust in what we were told rather than in how we feel. When we have only been *told* how to handle ourselves, our behavior can become automatic. Automatically we pick and choose. We learn to be perfect actors. It does not matter how we feel. We might be in tears, but still we put on a gleaming smile and make polite conversation. If we cannot find anything good to talk about, we just talk about the weather. With that approach, we become very crude. In fact, we are trying to become perfect actors rather than real people.

Some students of meditation have a similar problem. They have been told to keep a good posture and that the more a person keeps perfect posture, the closer he or she is to enlightenment. If one takes that approach without a sense of personal connection, it can produce a situation similar to that of the children of aristocracy who are taught to have good table manners. In both cases, there is a body problem, an actual physical problem, which has nothing to do with politics or society.

The tantric tradition is fundamentally an intentional approach to life in terms of how we handle our body. How we speak, how we look, how we touch our cup, our fork or knife, how we lift things and carry them about—all those things are very deliberate. But such deliberateness is not presented in a manual or book on how to act according to the tantric tradition. The point is that there is no such thing as a real tantric diet or proper tantric behavior. Instead, we develop a basic attitude, so that when we begin to extend our arm, we simply do it. When we begin to touch, we touch; and when we lift, we lift in a very confident way. We just do it. We have a real experience of confidence. There is no tantric finishing school, designed to train people for the tantric aristocracy or to develop a deceptive but well-mannered king. The tantric approach to body—how to handle our body and our sense perceptions, how to look, how to feel, how to listen, how to handle the whole situation—is very personal and real.

Tantra is deliberate, but at the same time, the heart of that deliberateness is freedom. The "crazy yogins" of the tantric tradition were not people who just hung out on street corners doing their crazy things. The freedom of tantra is something very real, dignified, and vajra-like. The sense of indestructibility is always there. There is intention, there is reality, and there are constant discoveries.

SECRET MANDALA

Then we have the third world, which is the secret mandala, or the mandala of the sacred realm. The sacredness and secretness of this mandala are not based on our being highly evolved and consequently looking down upon the outer mandala and the inner mandala. Rather, the secret mandala consists of simplifying our psychological behavior, our meditative behavior, into a sense of awareness and openness in which we have no hesitation, none whatsoever, in dealing with our emotions.

In the secret mandala emotions are all interwoven and interconnected. Passion is connected with aggression, aggression is connected with ignorance, ignorance is connected with envy or jealousy, and so forth. There is a continuous web taking place that is quite obvious and real. Therefore a person at the tantric level should not regard any *one* emotion as a big deal, but all emotions are a big deal. All the emotions that exist in a person's mind are the same problem— or the same promise, for that matter. They contain the seed of freedom, or liberation, and as well, the seed of imprisonment. In the secret mandala we work with all our hidden corners, any little areas of irritation. In fact, those things that we regard as little problems may actually be our biggest problems. Those problems are completely interrelated, which is the notion of mandala here.

There is a sense of continuity in our emotions and a sense of openness at the same time. For instance, we lose our temper, we become outraged, we are about to strangle our partner, and in fact we begin to do so—that itself is a mandala display. We feel angry, we feel passionate, we feel jealous, and we feel ignorant—all those things are happening at once. That is a real experience. There is no "how to do it"; we did it already. That is our chance. In fact, that is our golden opportunity. We have manifested the secret mandala already.

On the other hand, we usually do not acknowledge or experience our emotions properly. When we need release we might make love; when we need release we might kill someone. That is not quite the proper way to approach our emotions. Exploding on the spot is not the way to express emotions directly. Emotions are sacred; they should be regarded as real and obvious things that can teach us something. We should relate with them properly, without "getting off" on something or other. We might say, "I'm bored. Let's go to the movies." That is not quite the way to deal with our boredom.

The tantric approach to emotions is much more disciplined and much more personal. It is highly personal; that is why this mandala is called the sacred mandala. It is very difficult to achieve, but it is also very important and extremely sacred. Normally, no one is able to achieve such perfection, or even to conceive of such a possibility. So we should respect the sacredness of the secret mandala.

The mandala principle is an important concept in the tantric teachings. The outer mandala is connected with the external world: how to relate to society, politics, organizations, domestic relationships, and so forth. The inner mandala is connected with our body, and how to handle it. The secret mandala is connected with how to deal with our emotions. We have to incorporate all three mandala principles simultaneously in our experience. We can't separate them; we can't practice each of them separately, at different times. We have to do it all at once. In that way things become much more real.

The mandalas *are* reality. It is as simple as that. Of course, reality is real, but our contact with reality is through our sense perceptions, our body, and our emotions—the three mandalas. The three mandalas are what meet, or mate, with reality. When we put our finger on a hot stove, it is our perceptions that get burnt by their meeting with reality. We have to communicate with reality; otherwise, there is no reality. We might try to get out of the whole thing by saying, "Who cares?" But *that* becomes reality at the same time. We cannot get away from it. It is very personal, and it is very haunting. It is all over the place.

CHAPTER FOUR

Nontheistic Energy

Usually when we talk about energy, we are referring to an ongoing source of power, something that is able to generate power, such as an electric generator. In a similar manner, when we speak of an energetic person, we usually mean a vigorous person, someone who possesses enormous energy. When we are around such a person, we feel there is a bank of energy happening. That person works so hard that we feel guilty being idle around him or her. We feel that we should do something too, and we begin to work very hard. Then no one can say that we have been bad boys and girls, that we haven't done our chores, washed the dishes or ironed the sheets. Because we feel that person's enormous energy, we begin to perk up, and we stop being idle. We begin to take part in the energy.

Then there is another kind of energy, which is self-existing. Self-existing energy is not dependent on something or somebody else; it simply takes place continuously. Although the source of such energy is difficult to track down, it is universal and all-pervasive. It happens by itself, naturally. It is based on enthusiasm as well as freedom: enthusiasm in the sense that we trust what we are doing,

39

and freedom in the sense that we are completely certain that we are not going to be imprisoned by our own energy, but instead, freed constantly. In other words, we realize that such energy does come up by itself, and that we can work with it. This self-existing energy is the potentiality of *siddhi*, a Sanskrit word that refers to the ability to use the existing energies of the universe in a very special and appropriate way.

Self-existing energy is difficult to describe in words or concepts. When we try to describe this pattern of energy, we are only fingerpainting. Basically, it is the energy of the psychological realm. No matter what state of mind we are in, we experience a particular quality of life, that is, we experience an emotion. We begin to feel an electric spark taking place. That energy can come out of having a quarrel with our wife or out of having a severe accident or a love affair. It comes out of being either rejected or accepted.

This energy is created both when we fail to do something and when we accomplish something. Rejection or acceptance by the world does not mean that the energy is either invalid or valid. Rather, there is transparent energy happening all the time. Whether we are in an appropriate situation, in accordance with the laws of the universe, or we are in an inappropriate situation, not in accordance with the laws of the universe, energy is constantly taking place. This energy, from the vajrayana or tantric point of view, is simply the energy that exists. It does not mean being hard-working or extremely industrious, always doing things, being a busybody, or anything like that. This energy can come from all kinds of challenges, in the positive *or* negative sense. Such energy takes place constantly.

Self-existing energy permeates all of our emotional relationships: our emotions towards our relatives, our lovers, our friends, and our enemies. It also permeates our philosophical beliefs: either something is happening "right" according to our beliefs, or something has gone "wrong" according to our beliefs. Some situations try to dislodge us from our philosophical or religious commitments, and some situations try to draw us into certain commitments. All kinds of energies take place. So when we talk about energy, we are not talking about vigor alone but about that which exists in our lives. It is as though flint and steel were rubbing against each other and sparking constantly, again and again. That is, the phenomenal world exists, and we either rub against it or with it, and that rubbing is constantly creating a spark.

According to the tantric understanding of reality, energy is related to the experience of duality, the experience that you exist and others exist. Of course, both those concepts are false, but who cares about that?—at the time, anyway. The deceptive existence of you and other rubs together, nevertheless. Sometimes you are conquering the world and sometimes the world is conquering you. It is like riding on a balloon in the ocean: sometimes the balloon rides on you and you are underneath the ocean; sometimes you ride on the balloon and the balloon is underneath the ocean. That play of duality takes place constantly; that kind of electricity takes place all the time.

So the basic notion of energy is nothing particularly magical or miraculous. It is simply the rubbing together of the duality of you and the phenomenal world, you and other. We are talking about that spark, that fire. It is real fire, real water, real earth, and real air: the real elements are working with you. Still, at this point we have no idea who *you* are, actually. Let's just say we are talking about the basic *you*. Let's leave it vague at this point; otherwise it is going to get too complicated. Just leave it at *you*, this vague stuff that exists somewhere or other in the middle of the cosmos.

At this point the question arises of how we can handle, or utilize, such energy. In fact, that has been a question for a long, long time. For 2,500 years the same question has been asked: how can we handle self-existing energy; how can we work with it? Fundamentally, that question is the question of how to handle duality, or the basic split.

The split between self and other is taking place constantly, constantly creating energy, and we are always trying to work with it. Our approach is usually to try to unify the split in order to avoid the energy. We may say, "I am a good man; I am a bad man; I am Joe; I am Mary." In doing so, we are trying to bring self and other together in a superficial sense, as if no energy existed at all, as though everything were going smoothly: "There is nothing to worry about; everything's going to be okay. I am Mary, and that's smooth. There is no gap between *I* and *am* and *Mary* at all." Or we try to avoid the split by refusing to say "I am." Instead we might say, "My *name* is Mary." Still we have a problem. That approach of smoothing things out and trying to make everything presentable and respectable brings enormous problems, enormous questions. In fact, instead of getting rid of the energy, it raises further energy.

The attempt to define who we are and who we are not is basically split into two approaches: the theistic approach and the nontheistic approach. In the nontheistic approach we simply acknowledge the dualistic gap rather than trying to unify it or conceal it. In the theistic approach, there is an ongoing attempt to conceal that gap completely. There is a notion of spiritual democracy. In fact, that approach is often used in dealing with political and social problems: "Blacks are not against whites—we are all the same species. Since we all live on the same earth, we should regard ourselves as a brotherhood."

That approach of covering up separateness, pretending that the black man is a white man, is the cause of all kinds of problems; but the theistic approach can go much further than that, to the point of covering up *any* differences: "Let us have real unity. We can conceal this problem. We can iron it out completely, like a cloth. Let us work in such a way that when we have ironed our sheet we can even conceal the seams. In fact, we can make the whole sheet seem to be made out of one big cloth. God is in us and we are in God. It's all one, so don't worry."

Another way to cover the gap is to try to eliminate discomfort. The modern world has provided us with all sorts of conveniences: television, beautiful parents, lots of toys to play with, automobiles, and so on. There are notices everywhere offering entertainment and telling us how to handle ourselves. Even while we are flying in an airplane, we have food to entertain us. The world has provided all kinds of entertainment to make us feel better, to make sure that we do not feel bad or lonely. When we board an airplane, the stewardess says, "Welcome, ladies and gentlemen. I hope you have a comfortable flight. Call us if you need any help." That is a theistic remark, and such remarks occur all the time.

On the other hand, we could act without guidelines. This possibility may be completely unappealing to people who are used to their luxury. Nevertheless, it is a very truthful way to relate with things, and there is no room for deception. In this approach there is no hospitality; we have to provide our own hospitality. We have to work on ourselves. We are provided with kits, K-rations, booklets, and our own parachutes, and off we go. If we land on the top of a tree, we try to make the best of it; if we land in a gorge, we try to make the best of it. That is the nontheistic lifestyle: we can't do everything for one another. We have to make do for ourselves. We have to learn how to live with nature. So the nontheistic tradition is much harsher than the theistic tradition. It is very skeptical, unyielding, and somewhat outrageous.

We are not comparing Eastern and Western philosophies here, but theistic and nontheistic traditions, wherever they occur. We might hypothesize that Easterners think in a different way than Westerners, and that Eastern philosophy expresses this different style of thought. But philosophy is not that neatly divided into East and West. The basic thinking processes of the East and the West are the same. The only difference that exists is between the thinking style of ego and nonego. Failing to acknowledge that difference in style becomes a tremendous problem.

The standard approach to ecumenicism is to try to pretend that theism and nontheism are not different. But this is another theistic attempt to conceal the discomfort or the energy that comes from experiencing duality. We should be aware that differences exist. Then true ecumenicism, or continuity, can come about *because* of the differences.

In comparing theism and nontheism, we are discussing different approaches to separateness. In the theistic approach, we know that things are separate, but since we don't like it, we feel we should *do* something about it. We don't like the separateness; so we try to overcome it to the best of our ability, and that becomes an enormous problem. In the nontheistic approach, we also know that things are separate; therefore things are unified. Things are different, but that is not regarded as a problem. Fire is hot and water is cold, but still they can co-exist. Fire can boil water, changing it into steam, and water can kill fire. We should not be embarrassed about the functions of the universe.

We are still talking about energy—energy and reality. And we are concerned with what actual reality is. Is reality a gap, a crack, or is reality a big sheet of cloth, all-pervasive? In the nontheistic tradition of Buddhist tantra, when we begin to have a relationship with the world, we do not try to make sure that the world is part of us. In fact, the question of separation does not come up at all. According to the nontheistic tradition, we do not believe ourselves to be creatures. We are some kind of being—or nonbeing, for that matter—but we were never created, and therefore we are not particularly creatures. Nevertheless, there is a sense of continuity, without hysteria, without panic, without any congratulatory remarks or attempts to smooth things out. The world exists and we exist. We and the world are separate from that point of view—but so what? We could regard the separateness as part of the continuity rather than trying to deny it.

In the nontheistic approach, there is continuity, openness, and oneness—but in the sense of zeroness rather than even oneness. The nonexistence of a dualistic barrier does not quite mean that we are one, but that we are zero. Nontheism is the basis for understanding that. Tantra is continuity, so the thread of tantra runs through our life from beginning to end. In a sense, the beginning is part of the end, so a complete circle, or mandala, is formed. The beginning is the beginning of the end, and the end is the beginning of the beginning. That continuity is tantra. It is the continuous thread of openness that we could experience throughout our lives. Because of that, whatever sense perceptions or realms of experience come up, we can work through them.

From this point of view energy is very simple, extremely simple: energy is separate from you; therefore, energy is part of you. Without *you* separateness cannot exist. That is the dichotomy in Buddhist logic: you have form; therefore you do not have form. You cannot have form if you do not have formlessness, if you do not acknowledge or perceive formlessness. In the same way, you exist *because* you do not exist. Such riddles are regarded by Buddhists as the truth.

According to the tantric tradition of nontheism, energy is vital and important. Of course, in this approach we are viewing the world purely as a psychological process: if we do not have mind, we do not exist. The world comes out of our mind; it is created by our mind. From that point of view, working with energy, or developing *siddhi*, means that we do not have to depend on feedback but that we relate with life as straightforwardly and directly as possible. We relate directly to our domestic world, our enemies, our friends, our relatives, business partners, policemen, the government, or whatever happens in our life. We relate directly with energy as much as possible.

We are not talking about centralizing energy within ourselves, making ourselves into little atom bombs and then exploding. Working with energy in a tantric sense is a decentralized process. That is a very important point. We are talking about energy as something spreading, opening. Energy becomes all-pervasive. It is all and everywhere. If we centralize energy in ourselves, we are asking for trouble. We will find that we become like baby snakes who are vicious and angry but still very small. Or we may find that we are like extremely passionate, horny little baby peacocks. So it is important to remember that, in Buddhist tantra, energy is openness and all-pervasiveness. It is constantly expanding. It is decentralized energy, a sense of flood, ocean, outer space, the light of the sun and moon.

CHAPTER FIVE

Transmission

Our next topic is the transmission of vajrayana teachings from teacher to student. Before we can discuss transmission, however, it seems necessary to go back a step and examine our level of sanity and discipline. We need to examine what we have accomplished in our relationship with the world. If we have not been able to make a relationship with our suffering, frustrations, and neuroses, the feasibility of transmission is remote, extremely remote, for we have not even made a proper relationship with the most basic level of our experience.

I could say to you, "Forget all that. Forget your pain and suffering; it is going to be okay." I could give you all kinds of antidotes: tranquilizers, mantras, and tricks. I could say, "Soon you'll feel good. Soon you'll forget your pain, and then you'll be in a beautiful place." But that would be an enormous falsity, and in the long run, such an approach is ungenerous and extremely destructive to the spiritual path. It is like giving our children tranquilizers whenever they begin to misbehave so that they will fall asleep. It saves us the trouble of getting a babysitter and changing diapers, but the child becomes a complete zombie. That is not the human

thing to do, we must admit, and giving someone a spiritual tranquil-
izer is just as primitive as that. We suffer tremendously if we treat
spirituality in that way, and we have to pay for it later on. Enormous
problems arise—both resentment and discontent.

One approach that is used in presenting spirituality is to say
that if we have any questions, we should just forget them. We
should regard them as outside the circle of the spiritually initiated.
We should forget all our negativity: "Don't ask any questions; just
drop them. It is important that you have hope, that you go beyond
your questions. Only if you accept the whole thing will you be
saved." That strategy is used to take advantage of the sanity of
human beings—which is unlawful.

Someone may tell us that, if we commit ourselves to a particular
practice or path, within four weeks we are going to be okay; we
are going to be "high" forever. So we try it, and it works—but not
forever. After six weeks, at most, or perhaps after only ten days, we
begin to come down, and then we begin to panic and wonder what
is going on. Usually the most faithful students blame themselves,
feeling they have mismanaged the practice: "I must have some
problem that I haven't cleared up yet. I must not have done my
confession properly, or given in properly." But that is not the case at
all. The problem is the way they were indoctrinated into their
spiritual practice.

We accept what is presented to us with an open mind, which is
beautiful, but then its truth does not hold up. Because of the basic
deception involved in our initiation, all sorts of holes begin to
develop. Unfortunately, we become the victims of those lies, decep-
tions, or charlatanisms, and we feel the effects constantly, over and
over again.

So we have a problem with spiritual transmission, a problem of
how to get real transmission from a competent master into our
system. At this point, we are talking purely about the beginner's
level and the preparations that might be needed in order for spiritual transmission to occur in the very early stages. It is necessary for
us to sharpen our cynicism, to sharpen our whole critical attitude
towards what we are doing. That cynicism provides a basis for our
study and work. For instance, if we are building a bridge, we begin

by constructing the framework. It could be made of timber or iron rods, but the skeleton must be built before we pour the concrete. That is an example of the cynical approach. It is absolutely necessary to have that kind of cynical attitude if we are going to build a bridge, and it is necessary to be cynical in our approach to spirituality as well.

We need to encourage an attitude of constant questioning, rather than ignoring our intelligence, which is a genuine part of our potential as students. If students were required to drop their questions, that would create armies and armies of zombies—rows of jellyfish sitting next to each other. But, to use a local expression, that is not so neat. In fact, it is messy. Preparing a beautifully defined and critical background for what we are doing to ourselves and what the teaching is doing to us is absolutely important, *absolutely* important. Without that critical background, we cannot develop even the slightest notion or flavor of enlightenment.

Enlightenment is based on both *prajna*, or discriminating awareness, and compassion. But without cynicism, we do not have either. We do not have any compassion for ourselves because we are looking for something outside of ourselves, and we want to find the best way to get it. We also do not have any prajna, or clarity. We become completely gullible, and we are liable to be sucked in without any understanding, none whatsoever.

Transmission is like receiving a spiritual inheritance. In order to inherit our spiritual discipline, in order to have a good inheritance, we should become worthy vessels. In order to become worthy vessels, we have to drop the attitude that we are going to be saved, that there is going to be a magically painless operation, and that all we have to do is pay the doctor's fee. We have the notion that if we pay the doctor, everything will be taken care of. We can just relax and let him do what he wants. That attitude is simpleminded. It is absolutely necessary to think twice. The questioning mind is absolutely necessary; it is the basis of receiving transmission.

I am not stressing the importance of critical intelligence because Buddhism is just now being introduced to America and the West. It is not that I think students here might be more gullible. Buddhism is a strong tradition that has existed for 2,500 years, and throughout the ages students have been given these same instructions. Throughout the ages they have contributed their neuroses and their mistakes to help shape the methods and means of the Buddhist lineage. A learning process has been taking place for 2,500 years, in fact, even longer. And we have inherited all of that experience. So this approach is ages old rather than a sudden panic. It is an old way, very old and very traditional.

One of the responsibilities of the lineage holder is not to give an inch, but to keep up the tradition. At this point, tradition does not mean dressing up in robes and playing exotic music or having dakinis dancing around us, or anything like that. Tradition is being faithful to what we have been taught and to our own integrity. From this point of view, tradition is being awake and open, welcoming but at the same time stubborn.

According to tradition, the teacher should treat his students in this stubborn way: he should require that his students practice properly, in accordance with the tradition of the lineage. There are problems when a teacher is too kind to students who do not belong to the teacher's race and upbringing. Some teachers from the East seem to be excited by foreignness: "Wow! Finally we are going to teach the aliens, the overseas people." Because of this fascination and out of a naive generosity, they make unnecessary concessions. Although such teachers may be liberal enough to include Occidental students, to take them to heart and be very kind to them, their extraordinary kindness may be destructive.

Such teachers regard Westerners as an extraordinary species, as if they came from the planet Mars: "Well, why don't we teach them, since we have a captive audience of living Martians here?" That misunderstanding is an expression of limited vision, of failing to see that the world is one world made up of human beings. A person who lives on this earth needs food, shelter, clothing, a love affair, and so on. We are all alike in that regard. Westerners do not need any special treatment because they invented the airplane or electronics. All human beings have the same psychology: they think in the same way, and they have the same requirements as students. The question is simply how one can teach students no matter where they come from.

In that respect we can follow the example of the Buddha, who presented the teachings to the Indians of his time in a universal fashion. It is much more enlightened to view the world as one global situation. Everybody is united: we are all samsaric people, and we all have the potential to become enlightened as well. We do not have to be particularly kind towards one part of the world or another, or for that matter, aggressive towards one part of the world or another. We are one world; we share one earth, one water, one fire, and one sun.

Wherever a student comes from, his or her attitude is very important. To receive transmission, a student should be humble and open but not wretched. Being humble in this case is being like a teacup. If we are pouring a cup of tea, the cup could be said to be humble. The cup has a sense of being in its own place. When we pour tea into a cup, the cup is at a lower level and the pot is at a higher level. This has nothing to do with spiritual trips, higher consciousness, lower consciousness, or anything like that. We are talking pragmatically. If we are going to pour tea into a cup, the cup obviously should be lower than the pot. Otherwise we would be unable to pour anything into it.

Water obviously has to flow down. It is very simple. Like a humble cup, the student should feel fertile and at the same time open. Because tea is going to be poured into this particular cup, the cup has a sense of open expectation. Why not? We are no longer wretched people who are not up to the level of receiving teaching. We are simply students who want to know, who want to learn and receive instructions. Also, one cup is not necessarily better or more valuable than another. It could be made out of many things—ordinary clay, porcelain, gold, or silver—but it is still a cup as long as it can hold water or tea.

To be a proper cup, we should be free from spiritual materialism, thoroughly ripened, and brought to spiritual maturity so that transmission can take place. Then, in our basic being, we feel the quality of "cupness"; we feel our whole existence thirsting to receive teaching. We are open to the teachings. That is the first step in transmission: like the cup, we are on a certain level of experience that is not absolutely wretched or full of holes. We don't feel that we are deprived.

In fact, being a cup is an absolutely powerful thing: there is a sense of pride. Because our cup has such a strong quality of cupness, the teapot cannot help but fill it with knowledge or teachings. The teacher cannot wait to pour into us. We are seducing the teapot with our cupness: our pride, our self-existence, and our sanity. Two magnetic processes are taking place: the cup is magnetized by the teapot, and the teapot is equally magnetized by the cup. A love affair takes place; a fascination takes place.

Transmission means the extension of spiritual wakefulness from one person to someone else. Wakefulness is extended rather than transferred. The teacher, or the transmitter, extends his own inspiration rather than giving his experience away to somebody else and becoming an empty balloon. The teacher is generating wakefulness and inspiration constantly, without ever being depleted. So for the student, transmission is like being charged with electricity.

Transmission also requires the dynamic expression of the student's own emotions. As students, our aggression, our lust, and our stupidity are all included. According to vajrayana, everything we can think of, including the emotions, is workable. In fact, transmission cannot take place without emotions, because they are part of the food of transmutation. And since they are so energetic and powerful, we do not want to exclude any of them. As long as we separate our philosophy and our concepts of morality from our emotions, there is no problem. This does not mean that we should be completely loose, seemingly free from philosophy, morality, and ethics, but that self-existing ethics take place constantly. To receive transmission it is absolutely necessary to be an ordinary human being: confused, stupid, lustful, and angry. Without those emotional qualities, we cannot receive transmission. They are absolutely necessary. I do not think this is a particularly difficult requirement to fulfill. Everybody seems to have a pretty juicy helping of them.

Our emotions are regarded as the wiring or electrical circuit that receives transmission. We could say that we have three wires—one for passion, one for aggression, and one for naiveté, ignorance, or slothfulness. These three form a very busy electrical device that would like to receive transmission. We are hungry for it; we are dying for it. And on the other side, there is the electrical generator, which is somewhat smug, knowing that it is ready to transmit at any time.

So we have a good machine and we are beautifully wired: now we are just waiting for the generator to convey its charge—which in Sanskrit is called *abhisheka*. Abhisheka literally means "sprinkling," or "bathing," or "anointment." It is a formal ceremony of empowerment, a formal transmission from teacher to student. Abhisheka cannot take place unless the necessary wiring has already been set up, and to change our analogy slightly, abhisheka cannot take place without a good electrician, the teacher, or guru, who will know when to switch on the current.

In an abhisheka there is a sense of destruction, a sense of flow, and a sense of fulfillment. Those three principles of abhisheka are analogous to electricity in many ways: when we turn on a switch, the first thing that happens is that the resistance to the current is destroyed. Then, the current can flow through the circuit; and finally, the electricity can fulfill its purpose. If we turn on a lamp, first the electrical resistance is destroyed by turning on the switch, then the electricity flows, and finally the lamp is lit. In the same way, in receiving abhisheka destruction comes first, right at the beginning. Anything that is disorganized or confused and any misconceptions about receiving abhisheka get destroyed on the spot—immediately.

According to the tantric tradition, it is better not to get into tantra, but if we must get into it, we had better surrender. Having surrendered, we must give up the idea of survival. Survival means that we can still play our games, play our little tricks on the world. We have our usual routines, the little gadgets that we play with, the little colors that we pull out of our personality to make sure that we exist. But in tantra, it is not possible to play any games. So at the beginning it is necessary to give in completely. We have to surrender to groundlessness: there is no ground for us to develop security. As well we surrender to the fact that we cannot hold on to our ego, which by innuendo means that we surrender to the enlightened state of being. Then, actually, we do not have to do anything. Once we open, we just open.

All that is part of the first principle of abhisheka: destruction. When that first level of abhisheka takes place, it kills any unnecessary germs in our system. At that point, we have no hopes of manipulating anything at all. Then the flow of energy can take place. And after that, there is fulfillment: we finally begin to see the reality of what is possible in tantric experience. It is necessary for anyone involved with the discipline of vajrayana to understand the three principles of destruction, flow, and fulfillment. I am glad we could discuss these principles publicly, so that you will have a chance either to prepare yourselves or to run away. That creates a very open situation.

The student always has a chance to run away. We seem to have the concept that tantric discipline imposes itself on us, but what we are discussing is entirely self-imposed. The student might freak out at any time; he might feel weighted down, over-clean, and over-filled. But in order to receive transmission, he has to stay in his own place, which is not particularly pleasurable.

To conclude, the role of the guru in transmission is to electrify the student's vessel, so that it becomes clean and clear, free of all kinds of materialistic germs, and then to pour the essence into it. And if he is to be electrified at all, to be cleaned out and filled up, the student must be waiting and ready. He has to be willing to be made into a good vessel. As a good vessel, the student feels that he is opening and taking part constantly. And as a good vessel, he could hold all sorts of heavy-handed liquids. In a good vessel, we could drink alcoholic beverages; that is, we could drink up dualistic thoughts. We could drink the blood of ego, which is killed on the spot.

CHAPTER SIX

The Vajra Master

Many people have heard fascinating facts and figures about tantra, exciting stories about the "sudden path." Tantra may seem seductive and appealing, particularly when it seems to coincide with modern notions of efficiency and automation. If we ask people whether they prefer to walk up the stairs or ride in an elevator, most people, if they are not used to working hard, will say they prefer to ride in the elevator. But that attitude is a problem in relating to tantra. If students believe that tantra is supposed to be the quick path, then they think they should get quick results. They do not want to waste their time. Instead they want to get their money's worth, so to speak, and quickly become buddhas. They become impatient, and not only that, they become cowardly. They do not want to face pain or problems, because then they won't get quick results. With that attitude, students have very little willingness to expose themselves and to face the state of panic of the tantric practitioner.

The student of tantra should be in a constant state of panic. That panic is electric and should be regarded as worthwhile. Panic serves two purposes: it overcomes our sense of smugness and self-satisfaction, and it sharpens our clarity enormously. It has been said by Padma Karpo and other great tantric teachers that studying tantra is like riding on a razor blade. Should we try to slide down the razor blade or should we just try to sit still? If we know how to slide down the razor blade, we might do it as easily as a child slides down a bannister; whereas if we do not know the nature of the blade and we are just trying to prove our chauvinism, we might find ourselves cut in two. So the more warnings that are given about tantra, the more the student of tantra benefits. If the tantric master does not give enough warnings, the student cannot develop any real understanding of tantra at all, because he is not riding on the razor's edge.

Panic is the source of openness and the source of questions. Panic is the source of open heart and open ground. Sudden panic creates an enormous sense of fresh air, and that quality of openness is exactly what tantra should create. If we are good tantra students, we open ourselves each moment. We panic a thousand times a day, 108 times an hour. We open constantly and we panic constantly. That ongoing panic points to the seriousness of the tantric path, which is so overwhelmingly powerful and demanding that it is better *not* to commit ourselves to it. But if we *must* get into it, we should take it seriously—absolutely seriously.

It is possible that by following the tantric path we could develop vajra indestructibility and a sudden realization of enlightenment. But it is equally possible that we could develop an indestructible ego and find ourselves burnt up, as if we were an overcooked steak. We might find that we have become a little piece of charcoal. So there are two different possibilities: we could discover our inherent vajra nature, or we could become a piece of charcoal.

There is also a price on the head of the teacher. Those masters and teachers of tantra who teach students at the wrong time, who choose the wrong moment or say the wrong thing, or who are not able to experience accurately what is taking place may be condemned. They too may be reduced into pieces of charcoal. Such mistakes in teaching are called the offense of *sang drok* (*gsang-sgrogs*), which means declaring the secret at the wrong time. So there is a type of security system that has been set up in the vajrayana world.

If teachers feel that they can go outside the law, so to speak, outside the boundaries, or if they feel that they no longer need to commit themselves to the practice, they can be punished along with their students. It is because of this security system that the lineage of great tantric teachers has continued without interruption up to the present day. Everyone in the tantric lineage has panicked: the teachers have panicked and the students have panicked. Because of that healthy situation of panic, the tantric lineage has developed beautifully, smoothly, and healthily. Nobody has made mistakes. If anybody did make a mistake, he just vanished and became a piece of charcoal. Those who survived, both students and teachers, are those who developed vajra nature. Because of that they survived.

We might wonder why the vajrayana is kept secret at all. What is this famous tantric secret? The secret is not particularly exotic. It is not anything special. It simply refers to what we discover when we begin to play with the cosmos, the energy of the universe. As children we know that if we touch a naked wire we get a shock; we learn that by playing with our world. If we speed in our motor car we will crash. We know that much. Here we are talking about the spiritual equivalent of that knowledge, which is a hundred times worse or a hundred times more powerful, depending upon how we would like to put it. We are talking about the energy that exists in the world. We first have a glimpse of that energy, we get completely fascinated by it, and then we begin to play with it. We are asking for trouble, as any sensible person would tell us.

This warning has been given hundreds of times: "Don't get into tantra just like that. Start with hinayana, graduate to mahayana, and then you can become a tantric practitioner. If you have already done your homework and finished your basic training, then you can become a tantric practitioner. But even then, it is still dangerous." That has been said many hundreds of times. Every book written on tantra, every commentary, every tantric text that has been recorded in the history of the cosmos, begins with that warning: "Be careful; think twice; pay respect; don't just take this carelessly—be careful."

But interestingly enough, the more you put students off, the more interested they become.

The energy and power that exist in the tantric world are not different from what exists in the ordinary world. It is not that we suddenly wake up to a magical world. It is rather that developing a certain sensitivity exposes us to a different state of being. Often people who have taken hallucinogenic drugs claim that they have had a tantric experience, or people who have experienced extreme psychological depression or excitement claim that they have seen the tantric world. Those claims are somewhat suspicious.

When we talk about the tantric world, we are talking about *this* visual, auditory, sensory world, which has not been explored or looked at properly. Nobody has bothered to actually experience it. People just take it for granted. We may have been interested in our world when we were little children, but then we were taught how to handle it by our parents. Our parents already had developed a system to deal with the world and to shield themselves from it at the same time. As we accepted that system, we lost contact with the world. We lost the freshness and curiosity of our infancy a long time ago. And now, although the world is full of all kinds of things, we find that in communicating with the world we are somewhat numb. There is numbness in our sight, numbness in our hearing, numbness in all our senses. It is as though we had been drugged. The reality of the world—the brilliance of red, the brightness of turquoise, the majesty of yellow, and the fantastic quality of green—has not been seen properly. We have been indoctrinated, or we have indoctrinated ourselves. A state of numbness has developed, and we are not seeing our world properly.

The point of tantra is to reintroduce the world to us. Having developed a calmness of mind already in our practice of meditation, we can begin to re-view the world. We rediscover the world that exists around us, and we begin to find that this world is fabulous and fantastic. All kinds of exciting things are happening. Even people working nine-to-five jobs might find that their everyday life becomes fantastic. Every day is a different day rather than the same old thing.

The tantric approach to relating with the world is resharpening and reopening ourselves so that we are able to perceive our cosmos properly, thoroughly. We are keenly interested in and fascinated by the world. If we see a green light as we are driving, and it turns to amber and then red, it is fantastic. There is a world of self-existing messages and symbolism. For example, everybody dresses in his own colors and his own style of clothing. Some people decide to wear shirts and some people decide not to, but everybody wears a bottom part. Everybody has his own kind of hairdo. Some people wear glasses, and some do not. Everything makes sense. That is the whole point, that things make sense in their own right. Such truth does not have to be written in books—it is self-existing.

This may sound fantastic and enormously entertaining, but there is a catch. Along with that magic there is a naked sort of electricity. Once we are fascinated by this world and see the world without any filter or screen, then we are relating to the world so directly that it is as though we had no skin on our body. Experience becomes so intimate and so personal that it actually burns us or freezes us. It is not just that the world is becoming open to us, but we are shedding our skin as well. We may become extremely sensitive and jumpy people, and it is possible that we may panic more; we may react even more intensely. For instance, if we become too involved in the brightness of red, it could become poisonous. It is even possible that we could kill ourselves—cut our own throats.

The world is so magical that it gives us a direct shock. It is not like sitting back in our theater chair and being entertained by the fabulous world happening on the screen. It does not work that way. Instead it is a *mutual* process of opening between the practitioner and the world. Therefore tantra is very dangerous. It is electric and at the same time extremely naked. There is no place for our suit of armor. There is no time to insulate ourselves. Everything is too immediate. Our suit of armor is punctured from both outside and inside at once. Such nakedness and such openness reveal the cosmos in an entirely different way. It may be fantastic, but at the same time, it is very dangerous.

In addition to ourselves and the world, there is also a third element involved: the teacher who talks to us and introduces to us the possibility of such a true world. In the discipline of hinayana we relate to the teacher as a wise man who gives us constant instruction and guides us precisely. The relationship between teacher and student is very simple and clean-cut. In the discipline of mahayana, we regard the teacher as a *kalyanamitra* or spiritual friend, who works with us and relates to us as a friend. He guides us through the dangerous and the luxurious parts of the path; he tells us when to relax and when to exert ourselves, and he teaches the disciplines of helping others. In the discipline of vajrayana, the relationship between teacher and student is much more vigorous and highly meaningful. It is more personal and magical than consulting a sage or, for that matter, consulting a spiritual friend.

The vajrayana teacher is referred to as the vajra master. The vajra master is electric and naked. He holds a scepter in his hand, called a *vajra*, which symbolizes a thunderbolt. The teacher holds the power to conduct lightning with his hand. By means of the vajra he can transmit that electricity to us. If the cosmos and the student are not connecting properly, the vajra master can respark the connection. In this sense the teacher has a great deal of power over us, but not such that he can become an egomaniac. Rather, the teacher is a spokesman who reintroduces the world to us: he reintroduces us to our world.

The vajra master is like a magician in the sense that he has access to the cosmic world and can work with it, but not in the sense that he can turn earth into fire, or fire into water, just like that. The vajra master has to work with the actual functions of the universe. We could say that the cosmos contains a lot of magic, and because the vajra master has some connection with the world and the happenings of the world, there is magic already. Therefore, the vajra master could be considered a supervisor of magic rather than a magician.

Relating with the vajra master is extremely powerful and somewhat dangerous at this point. The vajra master is capable of transmitting the vajra spiritual energy to us, but at the same time, he is also capable of destroying us if our direction is completely wrong. Tantra means continuity, but one of the principles of tantric discipline is that continuity can only exist if there is something genuine to continue. If we are not genuine, then our continuity can be cancelled by the vajra master. So we do not regard our teacher in the vajrayana as a savior or as a deity who automatically will give us whatever we want.

The vajra master could be quite heavy-handed; however, he does not just play tricks on us whenever he finds a weak point. He conducts himself according to the tradition and the discipline: he touches us, he smells us, he looks at us, and he listens to our heartbeat. It is a very definite, deliberate process done according to the tradition of the lineage. That process—when the vajra master looks at us, when he listens to us, when he feels us, and when he touches us—is known as *abhisheka* or empowerment.

Abhisheka is sometimes translated as "initiation," but that does not actually convey the proper meaning. As we discussed earlier, abhisheka is a Sanskrit word that literally means "anointment." It is the idea of being bathed in holy water that is blessed by the teacher and the mandala around the teacher. However, abhisheka is not an initiation or rite of passage in which we are accepted as a member of the tribe if we pass certain tests. In fact, it is entirely different. The vajra master empowers us and we receive that power, depending both on our own capability and the capability of the teacher. Therefore the term "empowerment" is more appropriate than "initiation," because there is no tribe into which we are initiated. There is no closed circle; rather, we are introduced to the universe. We cannot say that the universe is a big tribe or a big ego; the universe is open space. So the teacher empowers us to encounter our enlarged universe. At this point the teacher acts as a lightning rod. We could be shocked or devastated by the electricity he transmits to us, but it is also possible that we could be saved by having such an electric conductor.

In the vajrayana, it is absolutely necessary to have a teacher and to trust in the teacher. The teacher or vajra master is the only embodiment of the transmission of energy. Without such a teacher we cannot experience the world properly and thoroughly. We cannot just read a few books on tantra and try to figure it out for ourselves. Somehow that does not work. Tantra has to be transmitted to the student as a living experience. The tantric system of working with the world and the energy of tantra have to be transmitted or handed down directly from teacher to student. In that way the teachings become real and obvious and precise.

A direct relationship between teacher and student is essential in vajrayana Buddhism. People cannot even begin to practice tantra without making some connection with their teacher, their vajra, indestructible, master. Such a teacher cannot be some abstract cosmic figure. He has to be somebody who has gone through the whole process himself—somebody who has been both a panicking student and a panicking teacher.

We could say that the vajra master exists because he is free from karma, but that through his compassion such a teacher establishes a relative link to his world. However, in a sense no one is actually free from karma, not even the enlightened buddhas. The buddhas are not going to retire from their buddhahood to some heavenly realm. They have to help us; they have to work with us. That is their karma and our karma as well.

That is one of the interesting differences between the theistic and the nontheistic approach. In the theistic approach, when we retire from this world, we go to heaven. Once we are in heaven we do not have anything to do with the world. We have no obligations, and we can be happy ever after. But in the nontheistic tradition, even if we attain the state of liberation or openness, we still have debts, because the rest of our brothers and sisters in the world are still in trouble. We have to come back. We can't just hang out in nirvana.

So the vajra master is a human being, someone who has a karmic debt to pay as a result of the intensity of his compassion. The dharma cannot be transmitted from the sun or the moon or the stars. The dharma can only be transmitted properly from human to human. So there is a need for a vajra master who has tremendous power—power over us, power over the cosmos, and power over himself—and who has also been warned that if he misdirects his energy he will be cut down and reduced into a little piece of charcoal.

It is extremely important to have a living vajra master, someone who personally experiences our pain and our pleasure. We have to have a sense of fear and respect that we are connecting and communicating directly with tantra. Making that connection is a very special thing. It is extremely difficult to find a true tantric situation and to meet a true tantric master. Becoming a true tantric student is also very difficult. It is very difficult to find the real thing.

CHAPTER SEVEN

Visualization

In tantra there is a sense of continuity, there is a sense of existence, and there is a sense of reality. If we are deeply involved in our experience, then there is a total and profound sense of experiencing reality. Whereas if we have a halfhearted approach to experience, then obviously we get halfhearted results in understanding reality. The tantric approach is complete involvement, which begins with a basic sense of being grounded: in our body, in our house, in our country, on this planet earth. We are not talking about taking trips to Mars or Jupiter or even to the moon. We are working right here, on this planet earth. Whether we like it or not, we are here and we have to face that.

This suggestion might seem rather depressing, if we do not want to keep relating with the earth. Of course, the earth has been glorified by descriptions of its beauty: the beautiful flowers and greenery that the earth nurtures, the waterfalls and rivers and fantastic mountains that the earth has provided. But apart from that, the earth seems to be rather hopeless. It is just a solid lump of rock.

We may try to cheer ourselves up by saying: "Wow! Fantastic! I took a trip to the Himalayas and I saw the beautiful mountains of

Kanchenjunga and Mount Kailas." Or we may say: "I saw the Rocky Mountains. I saw the Grand Canyon. Great!" Such remarks are just comic relief. In fact, we feel that we are stuck with this earth, and therefore we should glorify it; we should appreciate it. But deep in our hearts, we would like to take off. We would like to fly away into the cosmos, into outer space. We really would like to do that. In particular, anyone seeking spiritual materialism or spiritual entertainment feels that way: "Wouldn't it be much better if we could leave this earth, our home ground, if we could swim across the galaxies of stars? We could feel the cosmos bubbling, and we could dance in the darkness, and occasionally we would relate with the sun or the planets." The problem with that approach is that we want to neglect our home ground and the familiarity of our highways, our plastic world, our pollution, and all the mundane happenings in our lives. But they are all part of the adornment of living on this earth—whether we like it or not.

What is familiar becomes a part of tantric study, because it is basic to our state of being. Our state of being is grounded in a sense of continual experience, a sense of continual landmarks of all kinds. For instance, our body is a landmark. It marks the fact that we were born on this earth. We do not have to refer back to our birth certificate to make sure that we were born. We know that we are here, our name is such and such, our parents are so and so. We were born in Louisiana, Texas, Colorado, New York City, Great Neck, or wherever. We were born, and we were raised in our hometown. We went to school and studied and did our homework. We related with other people: we began to play and to fight with the other students, and we began to develop into real boys or girls. Eventually we went to a bigger school, called a university. Then we really began to grow up: we began to take part in politics and philosophy and to experiment with life. We developed opinions of all kinds. Finally we grew up and became men and women—real individuals. Now we are people of the world. As grownups, we might be looking for marriage partners or business contacts, or we might be dropping out of the world and becoming free spokesmen, who do not believe in this crazy society. In any case, as men and women of the world, we make our statements; we develop our philosophy. In tantric language, that experience is called *samaya*.

Samaya is a basic term in the language of tantra. The Tibetan translation *tamtsik (dam-tshig)*, literally means "sacred word." The fact of life, the actual experience of life, is samaya. Whatever we decide to do, all the trips we go through, all the ways we try to become an individual are personal experience. Fighting for personal rights of all kinds, falling in love or leaving our lover, relating with our parents, making political commitments, relating with our job or our church—all these things are the expression of samaya.

At a certain point in our life, we begin to live on our own. We may try to reject any interdependence as fast and as hard as we can. Although it is impossible to be completely independent, we still try to be so. We try to get any factors out of our system that seem to bind us. We feel that we have been imprisoned by our parents, by society, by the economy, or by our religion. So we try to get out of those prisons and we try to get into expressing our personal freedom. On the other hand, rather than rebelling, we might choose to get into a certain church or a particular social environment based on a sense of our own personal choice. That could also express our freedom, because we were never told to do that—we just decided personally to do it. When we commit ourselves to the world, whether as a reaction to constraints or as a decision to get into something new, that is called samaya, sacred word, or sacred vow.

Whether we are pushed, and we begin to give in and then slowly we get into the system, or whether we are pushed and we reject the system completely, that is an expression of independence in our personal mental functioning. Any move we make to join a society, organization, or church is based on our own personal experience rather than just tradition or history. On the other hand, breaking away from anything that we feel entraps us is also based on personal experience. Therefore, the commitments and choices that we make are called sacred word, or sacred bondage—which are saying the same thing. Samaya can be interpreted as sacred bondage, although literally it means sacred word, because we are bound by certain norms, certain processes that organize our experience.

When we accept those boundaries as our own, that is the sacred bondage of samaya.

In the tantric practice of visualization, we visualize what is known as the *samayasattva*. *Sattva* literally means "being," "individual" or "person." *Samaya*, as we discussed, means acknowledging connections and being willing to bow down to the experience of life. Sattva is the being who experiences the situation of samaya. So in visualizing the samayasattva we are acknowledging our experience of life and our willingness to commit ourselves to it. We acknowledge that we are willing to enter fully into life.

Visualization is a central practice of tantra. It not only encompasses visual perception, but it is also a way of relating with all sense perceptions—visual, auditory, tactile, mental—with the entire range of sensory experience, all at the same time. As well, it should be obvious from our discussion of samaya that visualization is a way of relating to our state of mind and a way of working with our experience.

In order to begin the tantric practice of visualization, we must have gone through the disciplines of hinayana and mahayana already, and we must have done preliminary vajrayana practices as well. Then when we receive abhisheka, we are given a deity to visualize, a samayasattva connected with our own makeup, our basic being. Whether we are an intellectual person, or an aggressive person, or a passionate person, or whatever we are, in accordance with our particular qualities, a certain deity is given to us by our vajra master, who knows us personally and is familiar with our particular style. The deity that we visualize or identify with is part of our makeup. We may be outrageously aggressive, outrageously passionate, outrageously proud, outrageously ignorant, or outrageously lustful—whatever our basic makeup may be, that complex of emotions is connected with enlightenment. None of those qualities or emotional styles are regarded as obstacles. They are related with our personal experience of a sense of being, a sense of existence. If we must exist in lust, let us abide in our lust; if we must exist in anger, let us abide in our anger. Let us live in our anger. Let us do it. Let us be that way.

Therefore, we visualize a deity that is connected with our own particular qualities and our commitment to ourselves and to our experience. Having visualized that deity, called the samayasattva of our basic being, then we invite what is known as the *jnanasattva*. The jnanasattva is another being or level of experience that we are inviting into our system; however, it is nothing particularly extraordinary or fantastic. *Jnana* is a state of wakefulness or openness, whereas samaya is an experience of bondage, or being solidly grounded in our experience. The samayasattva is basically at the level of body and speech, whereas the jnanasattva is an awakening quality that comes from beyond that level. Jnanasattva is the quality of openness or a sense of cosmic principle. At the same time, jnana is a fundamentally cynical attitude towards life, which is also a humorous attitude.

In this case humor does not mean being nasty or making fun of people. Instead it is constantly being fascinated and amused in a positive sense. We may be amused at how somebody eats his spaghetti. He does it in such a personal way, and the way he eats his spaghetti seems to be very healthy and, at the same time, humorous. It is not that the person is funny in a cheap sense, but that person has the courage to eat his spaghetti in a direct and beautiful way. He actually tastes the spaghetti, and he uses it properly, productively. There is a sense of healthiness in seeing that person handle his universe properly.

Jnana is experiencing a feeling of humor and fascination about everything and realizing that everything is being handled properly— even on the inanimate level. Flowers grow, rocks sit, pine trees are there. These things are unique, personal, and very real. So the humor of jnana is entirely different from the basic bondage of samaya. With jnana there is a real feeling of upliftedness and appreciation. When we see somebody doing something, we appreciate that he is not just conducting his affairs, but he conducts them fully, artfully, and humorously.

Jnana literally means "wisdom" or, more accurately, "being wise." Wisdom implies an entity, a body of wisdom that we could learn or experience, such as "the wisdom of the ages." But jnana is the *state* of being wise, a spontaneous and personal state of experience. In the term *jnanasattva, jnana* is this state of wisdom, and *sattva* again is "being." But in this case sattva expresses the sense of being at a humorous and open level.

The goal in all tantric traditions is to bring together the lofty idea, the jnanasattva of humor and openness, with the samayasattva, which is the bodily or physical orientation of existence. The practice of visualization is connected with that process of combining the jnanasattva and the samayasattva. In a sense, the level of jnanasattva is free from visualization. We do not have to visualize jnanasattvas as such: they just come along. They just float down from the sky and join our own cluttered and clumsy visualization; they simply dissolve into our clutteredness.

CHAPTER EIGHT

Body, Speech, and Mind

An important principle in the tantric tradition is the role of body, speech, and mind in our relationship with the cosmos or the world. The vajrayana teachings place great importance on these principles. In fact, the notion of vajra nature is developing vajra—indestructible—body, vajra speech, and vajra mind. We all have certain ideas about what body is, what speech is, and what mind is, but we should examine the tantric understanding, which could be quite different from our ordinary associations.

The sensory world of the body obviously includes shapes, colors, and sounds. That is quite simple. We all know that. At the same time, the body has a divine or transcendental aspect. There is a transcendental aspect because bodies are not really bodies, shapes are not really shapes, and sounds, sights, colors, and touchable objects are not really there. At the same time they *are* actually there. That kind of phenomenal play between existence and nonexistence takes place all the time, and we are pushed back and forth. In general, either we say that we are *not* there and we hold onto that particular metaphysical argument, or else we say that we *are* there and we try to hold onto *that* metaphysical standpoint. But in

71

tantra we cannot hold onto either of those views. We cannot hold onto any of our sense perceptions or experiences.

Things are there because they are not there—otherwise they could not exist. They are there because they are dependent on their nonexistence. Things cannot exist unless they can not-exist. A white poodle crossing the highway is *not* a white poodle because her whiteness depends on blackness. Therefore the white poodle *is* a white poodle because the whiteness depends on blackness. A white poodle crossing the highway is definitely a white poodle because she is not a black poodle. At the same time there is no highway. It is very simple logic; in fact it is simpleminded: the crescent moon is a crescent moon because it is not a full moon. But on the basis of that very simple logic we can build fascinating and sophisticated logic: I exist because I do not exist; you exist because you do not exist; I exist and you exist because I do not exist; and you and I exist because we do not exist. To understand that type of logic requires training, but it is actually true. Once we look into that system of thinking, the sun is black because it is bright, daytime is nighttime because it is daytime, and so forth.

The experience of body or shape or form is usually such a hassle for us that we cannot solve problems of logic. At the tantric level, the logic of believing in being or form, believing in the actuality of physically existing here right now—I have my body and I am fat or I am thin—begins to become a problem, and at the same time, it becomes a source of study. The body exists because of its bodyness. That might be our psychological attitude. But when we again ask what bodyness is, we discover it is nonbodyness. We cannot find an answer, because answers always run out. That is both the problem and the promise.

The vajra mandala of body refers to that back-and-forth play: things are seemingly there, but at the same time they are questionable. That play gives us enormous ground to work with. We do not have to work our hearts and brains to their extreme limits so that we finally become mad professors of tantra. Instead we can work and relate with that play of experience. At the level of the vajra mandala of body, our experience of the world becomes entirely phenomenological. It is a much more personal experience than even existentialists talk about. It is entirely phenomenological, and yet it transcends the notion of phenomenological experience, because the phenomena do not actually exist.

Next is the role of speech. We are considering speech from the same phenomenological perspective as body. We are taking the same logical stance, but we are approaching our experience from a slightly different angle. At the level of speech, there is much more movement, much more shiftiness and dancelike quality than in our experience of the body. The vajra mandala of speech refers to the mandala of letters, which are traditionally seen as symbols and seed syllables. Relating to the mandala of letters does not mean being literate, or being an educated person. Instead it is the notion of seeing the world in terms of letters: A-B-C-D. The phenomenal world actually spells itself out in letters and even sentences that we read, or experience.

Through the mandala of speech, the world is seen as a world of syllables, a world of letters. My friend is made out of A. My lover is made out of B-X. My sister is made out of B-B. My brother is made out of B-A. Everybody has his own symbol. Everything stands for its own point of reference, which we can read. But at the same time it is a subtle language. Today is a B-day because the sun is shining and it is hot. Tomorrow might be an X-day if it is raining. The next day might be a Y-day if it is partly cloudy and partly clear. Or, today is an extremely K-day because it is so cold and snowy. Hopefully tomorrow will be an N-day, which is partially warm and partially cold. The entire world, every experience, is made out of letters from that point of view. According to tantric Sanskrit literature, the world is made up of fourteen vowels and thirty-three consonants. But we have to have a personal experience of that.

Understanding the mandala of speech is basic to how we raise children. From the beginning of their infancy, children begin to read us. They read mommy, they read daddy, and they read how we handle ourselves. They read us opening a bottle or a can. They read how we undo a box of chocolates. They can read the world in the same way that we do. The whole process starts right at the begin- ning, in infancy. We were all children once upon a time. In fact we still may be children in some sense, because we are all learning to read the world. We learn to read books; we learn to read highways; we learn to read motor cars; we learn to read our own minds. Reading takes place constantly. Because we read a face, the next time we see someone we recognize that person; because they also read us, they know who we are as well. In the same way that we read books, we read each other. We read constantly.

But a problem occurs when we do not have any new reading material and when the reading material that we already have has been memorized by heart. When something is interesting or challenging to us, we don't just skip over it quickly; we pause to read carefully. But when we find that we are reading something familiar, we are dying to get on to the next paragraph, and we rush. We are constantly looking for entertainment. We don't really want to read the pages of life properly and we panic; we actually panic tremendously. From the tantric perspective, that panic is called neurosis. We run out of reading material and we panic. Or we begin to find spelling mistakes. When we finally become smart enough to notice them, we cease to take a humorous attitude and we begin to panic. We begin to criticize the editor of the journal of the world.

On the spiritual level, when people experience the neurosis of speech, sometimes they think they have opened their sound cakras: "Now I can be verbose and accurate in what I have to say, and I can speak very fast." But there is some kind of problem with that approach; it is actually a reading impediment. When somebody has opened his sound cakra he does not have to speak so fast. He does not have to write poetry suddenly or become a completely verbose person. There is something fishy about that, something sacrilegious. That is disregarding the world-mandala of letters and syllables.

Next is the level of mind. Mind in this case is very simple; in fact, it is simplemindedness. We are not talking about the mind that thinks, but the mind that feels in a haphazard way. Such mind does not depend on whether we are educated or not. We are simply talking about the mind that feels different things in different ways. On the naive or ignorant level, the functioning of mind brings an experience of nonexistence in the negative sense. We are afraid, and we do not have enough guts to realize that the phenomenal world is magical. At the tantric level, the positive experience of nonexistence comes about when the mind is completely tuned into the magical possibilities of life. At the level of the vajra mandala of mind, subconscious gossip, or the continual background chatter and ongoing commentary of our thoughts, is completely cut through. Mind is completely open. This vajra experience of mind creates a continuous celebration in dealing with life directly and simply. At the vajra level of mind, every situation takes place very simply, on its own, and mind relates with whatever arises quite simply.

CHAPTER NINE

The Five Buddha Families

Tantra is extraordinarily special, and extremely real and personal. The question in this chapter is how to relate our own ordinary existence or daily situation to tantric consciousness. The tantric approach is not just to make sweeping statements about reality and to create calmness and a meditative state. It is more than learning to be creative and contemplative. In tantra we relate with the details of our everyday life according to our own particular make-up. It is a real and personal experience. But in order to relate to our lives in the tantric fashion, there are certain technical details of tantric experience that we have to understand.

The tantric discipline of relating to life is based on what are known as the five buddha principles, or the five buddha families. These principles are traditionally known as families because they are an extension of ourselves in the same way that our blood relations are an extension of us: we have our daddy, we have our mommy, we have our sisters and brothers, and they are all part of our family. But we could also say that these relatives are principles: our motherness, our fatherness, our sisterness, our brotherness, and our me-ness are experienced as definite principles that have distinct characteristics.

In the same way, the tantric tradition speaks of five families: five principles, categories, or possibilities.

Those five principles or buddha families are called *vajra*, *ratna*, *padma*, *karma*, and *buddha*. They are quite ordinary. There is nothing divine or extraordinary about them. The basic point is that at the tantric level people are divided into particular types: vajra, ratna, padma, karma, and buddha. We constantly come across members of every one of the five families—people who are partially or completely one of those five. We find such people all through life, and every one of them is a fertile person, a workable person who could be related with directly and personally. So, from the tantric point of view, by relating directly with all the different people we encounter, we are actually relating with different styles of enlightenment.

The buddha family, or families, associated with a person describes his or her fundamental style, that person's intrinsic perspective or stance in perceiving the world and working with it. Each family is associated with both a neurotic and an enlightened style. The neurotic expression of any buddha family can be transmuted into its wisdom or enlightened aspect. As well as describing people's styles, the buddha families are also associated with colors, elements, landscapes, directions, seasons—with any aspect of the phenomenal world.

The first buddha family is the *vajra* family, which literally means the family of sharpness, crystallization, and indestructibility. The term vajra is superficially translated as "diamond," but that is not quite accurate. Traditionally, vajra is a celestial precious stone that cuts through any other solid object. So it is more than a diamond; it is complete indestructibility. The vajra family is symbolized by the vajra scepter, or dorje in Tibetan. This vajra scepter or super-diamond has five prongs, which represent relating to the five emotions: aggression, pride, passion, jealousy, and ignorance. The sharp edges or prongs of the vajra represent cutting through any neurotic emotional tendencies; they also represent the sharp quality of being aware of many possible perspectives. The indestructible vajra is said to be like a heap of razor blades: if we naively try to hold it or touch it, there are all kinds of sharp edges that are both cutting and penetrating. The notion here is that vajra corrects or remedies any neurotic distortion in a precise and sharp way.

In the ordinary world, the experience of vajra is perhaps not as extreme as holding razor blades in our hand, but at the same time, it is penetrating and very personal. It is like a sharp, cutting, biting-cold winter. Each time we expose ourselves to the open air, we get frostbite instantly. Intellectually vajra is very sharp. All the intellectual traditions belong to this family. A person in the vajra family knows how to evaluate logically the arguments that are used to explain experience. He can tell whether the logic is true or false. Vajra family intellect also has a sense of constant openness and perspective. For instance, a vajra person could view a crystal ball from hundreds of perspectives, according to where it was placed, the way it was perceived, the distance from which he was looking at it, and so forth. The intellect of the vajra family is not just encyclopedic; it is sharpness, directness, and awareness of perspectives. Such indestructibility and sharpness are very personal and very real.

The neurotic expression of vajra is associated with anger and intellectual fixation. If we become fixated on a particular logic, the sharpness of vajra can become rigidity. We become possessive of our insight, rather than having a sense of open perspective. The anger of vajra neurosis could be pure aggression or also a sense of uptightness because we are so attached to our sharpness of mind. Vajra is also associated with the element of water. Cloudy, turbulent water symbolizes the defensive and aggressive nature of anger, while clear water suggests the sharp, precise, clear reflectiveness of vajra wisdom. In fact, vajra wisdom is traditionally called the Mirrorlike Wisdom, which evokes this image of a calm pond or reflecting pool.

Incidentally, the use of the term *vajra* in such words as vajrayana, vajra master, and vajra pride does not refer to this particular buddha family, but simply expresses basic indestructibility.

The next buddha family is *ratna*. Ratna is a personal and real sense of expanding ourselves and enriching our environment. It is expansion, enrichment, plentifulness. Such plentifulness could also have problems and weaknesses. In the neurotic sense, the richness of ratna manifests as being completely fat, or extraordinarily ostentatious, beyond the limits of our sanity. We expand constantly, open heedlessly, and indulge ourselves to the level of insanity. It is like swimming in a dense lake of honey and butter. When we coat ourselves in this mixture of butter and honey, it is very difficult to remove. We cannot just remove it by wiping it off, but we have to apply all kinds of cleaning agents, such as cleanser and soap, to loosen its grasp.

In the positive expression of the ratna family, the principle of richness is extraordinary. We feel very rich and plentiful, and we extend ourselves to our world personally, directly, emotionally, psychologically, even spiritually. We are extending constantly, expanding like a flood or an earthquake. There is a sense of spreading, shaking the earth, and creating more and more cracks in it. That is the powerful expansiveness of ratna.

The enlightened expression of ratna is called the Wisdom of Equanimity, because ratna can include everything in its expansive environment. Thus ratna is associated with the element of earth. It is like a rotting log that makes itself at home in the country. Such a log does not want to leave its homeground. It would like to stay, but at the same time, it grows all kinds of mushrooms and plants and allows animals to nest in it. That lazy settling down and making ourselves at home, and inviting other people to come in and rest as well, is ratna.

The next family is *padma*, which literally means "lotus flower." The symbol of the enlightened padma family is the lotus, which grows and blooms in the mud, yet still comes out pure and clean, virginal and clear. Padma neurosis is connected with passion, a grasping quality and a desire to possess. We are completely wrapped up in desire and want only to seduce the world, without concern for real communication. We could be a hustler or an advertiser, but basically, we are like a peacock. In fact, Amitabha buddha, the buddha of the padma family, traditionally sits on a peacock, which represents subjugating padma neurosis. A person with padma neurosis speaks gently, fantastically gently, and he or she is seemingly very sexy, kind, magnificent, and completely accommodating: "If you hurt me, that's fine. That is part of our love affair. Come towards me." Such padma seduction sometimes becomes excessive and sometimes becomes compassionate, depending on how we work with it.

Padma is connected with the element of fire. In the confused state, fire does not distinguish among the things it grasps, burns, and destroys. But in the awakened state, the heat of passion is transmuted into the warmth of compassion. When padma neurosis is transmuted, it becomes fantastically precise and aware; it turns into tremendous interest and inquisitiveness. Everything is seen in its own distinct way, with its own particular qualities and characteristics. Thus the wisdom of padma is called Discriminating Awareness Wisdom.

The genuine character of padma seduction is real openness, a willingness to demonstrate what we have and what we are to the phenomenal world. What we bring to the world is a sense of pleasure, a sense of promise. In whatever we experience, we begin to feel that there is lots of promise. We constantly experience a sense of magnetization and spontaneous hospitality.

This quality of padma is like bathing in perfume or jasmine tea. Each time we bathe, we feel refreshed, fantastic. It feels good to be magnetized. The sweet air is fantastic and the hospitality of our host is magnificent. We eat the good food provided by our host, which is delicious, but not too filling. We live in a world of honey and milk, in a very delicate sense, unlike the rich but heavy experience of the ratna family. Fantastic! Even our bread is scented with all kinds of delicious smells. Our ice cream is colored by beautiful pink lotus-like colors. We cannot wait to eat. Sweet music is playing in the background constantly. When there is no music, we listen to the whistling of the wind around our padma environment, and it becomes beautiful music as well. Even though we are not musicians, we compose all kinds of music. We wish we were a poet or a fantastic lover.

The next family is the *karma* family, which is a different kettle of fish. In this case we are not talking about karmic debts, or karmic consequences; *karma* in this case simply means "action." The neurotic quality of action or activity is connected with jealousy, comparison, and envy. The enlightened aspect of karma is called the Wisdom of All-Accomplishing Action. It is the transcendental sense of complete fulfillment of action without being hassled or pushed into neurosis. It is natural fulfillment in how we relate with our world. In either case, whether we relate to karma family on the transcendental level or the neurotic level, karma is the energy of efficiency.

If we have a karma family neurosis, we feel highly irritated if we see a hair on our teacup. First we think that our cup is broken and that the hair is a crack in the cup. Then there is some relief. Our cup is not broken; it just has a piece of hair on the side. But then, when we begin to look at the hair on our cup of tea, we become angry all over again. We would like to make everything very efficient, pure, and absolutely clean. However, if we do achieve cleanliness, then that cleanliness itself becomes a further problem: we feel insecure because there is nothing to administer, nothing to work on. We constantly try to check every loose end. Being very keen on efficiency, we get hung up on it.

If we meet a person who is not efficient, who does not have his life together, we regard him as a terrible person. We would like to get rid of such inefficient people, and certainly we do not respect them, even if they are talented musicians or scientists or whatever they may be. On the other hand, if someone has immaculate efficiency, we begin to feel that he is a good person to be with. We would like to associate ourselves exclusively with people who are both responsible and clean-cut. However, we find that we are envious and jealous of such efficient people. We want others to be efficient, but not more efficient than we are.

The epitome of karma family neurosis is wanting to create a uniform world. Even though we might have very little philosophy, very little meditation, very little consciousness in terms of developing ourselves, we feel that we can handle our world properly. We have composure, and we relate properly with the whole world, and we are resentful that everybody else does not see things in the same way that we do. Karma is connected with the element of wind. The wind never blows in all directions but it blows in one direction at a time. This is the one-way view of resentment and envy, which picks on one little fault or virtue and blows it out of proportion. With karma wisdom, the quality of resentment falls away but the qualities of energy, fulfillment of action, and openness remain. In other words, the active aspect of wind is retained so that our energetic activity touches everything in its path. We see the possibilities inherent in situations and automatically take the appropriate course. Action fulfills its purpose.

The fifth family is called the *buddha* family. It is associated with the element of space. Buddha energy is the foundation or the basic space. It is the environment or oxygen that makes it possible for the other principles to function. It has a sedate, solid quality. Persons in this family have a strong sense of contemplative experience, and they are highly meditative. Buddha neurosis is the quality of being "spaced-out" rather than spacious. It is often associated with an unwillingness to express ourselves. For example, we might see that our neighbors are destroying our picket fence with a sledge hammer. We can hear them and see them; in fact, we have been watching our neighbors at work all day, continuously smashing our picket fence. But instead of reacting, we just observe them and then we return to our snug little home. We eat our breakfast, lunch, and dinner and ignore what they are doing. We are paralyzed, unable to talk to outsiders.

Another quality of buddha neurosis is that we couldn't be bothered. Our dirty laundry is piled up in a corner of our room. Sometimes we use our dirty laundry to wipe up spills on the floor or table and then we put it back on the same pile. As time goes on, our dirty socks become unbearable, but we just sit there.

If we are embarking on a political career, our colleagues may suggest that we develop a certain project and expand our organization. If we have a buddha neurosis, we will choose to develop the area that needs the least effort. We do not want to deal directly with the details of handling reality. Entertaining friends is also a hassle. We prefer to take our friends to a restaurant rather than cook in our home. And if we want to have a love affair, instead of seducing a partner, talking to him or her and making friends, we just look for somebody who is already keen on us. We cannot be bothered with talking somebody into something.

Sometimes we feel we are sinking into the earth, the solid mud and earth. Sometimes we feel good because we think we are the most stable person in the universe. We slowly begin to grin to ourselves, smile at ourselves, because we are the best person of all. We are the only person who manages to stay stable. But sometimes we feel that we are the loneliest person in the whole universe. We do not particularly like to dance, and when we are asked to dance with somebody, we feel embarrassed and uncomfortable. We want to stay in our own little corner.

When the ignoring quality of buddha neurosis is transmuted into wisdom, it becomes an environment of all-pervasive spaciousness. This enlightened aspect is called the Wisdom of All-Encompassing Space. In itself it might still have a somewhat desolate and empty quality, but at the same time, it is a quality of completely open potential. It can accommodate anything. It is spacious and vast like the sky.

In tantric iconography, the five buddha families are arrayed in the center and the four cardinal points of a mandala. The mandala of the five buddha families of course represents their wisdom or enlightened aspect. Traditionally, the buddha family is in the center. That is to say, in the center there is the basic coordination and basic wisdom of buddha, which is symbolized by a wheel and the color white. Vajra is in the East, because vajra is connected with the dawn. It is also connected with the color blue and is symbolized by the vajra scepter. It is the sharpness of experience, as in the morning when we wake up. We begin to see the dawn, when light is first reflected on the world, as a symbol of awakening reality.

Ratna is in the South. It is connected with richness and is symbolized by a jewel and the color yellow. Ratna is connected with the midday, when we begin to need refreshment, nourishment. Padma is in the West and is symbolized by the lotus and the color red. As our day gets older, we also have to relate with recruiting a lover. It is time to socialize, to make a date with our lover. Or, if we have fallen in love with an antique or if we have fallen in love with some clothing, it is time to go out and buy it. The last family is karma, in the North. It is symbolized by a sword and the color green. Finally we have captured the whole situation: we have everything we need, and there is nothing more to get. We have brought our merchandise back home or our lover back home, and we say, "Let's close the door; let's lock it." So the mandala of the five buddha families represents the progress of a whole day or a whole course of action.

Without understanding the five buddha families, we have no working basis to relate with tantra, and we begin to find ourselves alienated from tantra. Tantra is seen as such an outrageous thing, which seems to have no bearing on us as individuals. We may feel the vajrayana is purely a distant aim, a distant goal. So it is necessary to study the five buddha principles. They provide a bridge between tantric experience and everyday life.

It is necessary to understand and relate with the five buddha principles *before* we begin tantric discipline, so that we can begin to understand what tantra is all about. If tantra is a mystical experience, how can we relate it to our ordinary everyday life at home? There could be a big gap between tantric experience and day-to-day life. But it is possible, by understanding the five buddha families, to close the gap. Working with the buddha families we discover that we already have certain qualities. According to the tantric perspective, we cannot ignore them and we cannot reject them and try to be something else. We have our aggression and our passion and our jealousy and our resentment and our ignorance—or whatever we have. We belong to certain buddha families already, and we cannot reject them. We should work with our neuroses, relate with them and experience them properly. They are the only potential we have, and when we begin to work with them, we see that we can use them as stepping stones.

CHAPTER TEN

Abhisheka

In an earlier chapter we discussed the basic meaning of transmission. At this point we could go further in our understanding and discuss some of the details. Basically, transmission is the meeting of two minds. Understanding this is absolutely necessary. Otherwise, there is no way out and no way in—there is no way to enter the vajrayana, even if we have already been trained in the basic Buddhist teachings. The formal experience of transmission takes place at a ceremony, which is called an *abhisheka*. The particular form of the abhisheka that we receive is suited to our own basic being or basic psychological state, and it also depends on the particular level of tantric practice that is appropriate for us. So altogether there is a need to respect the nature of transmission itself, the form of transmission, and also a need to respect our own attitude in receiving transmission.

In order to receive transmission, we must be willing to commit ourselves to the fundamental trust, or the potential for trust, that exists as the working basis of the student-teacher relationship. This attitude of trust is extremely important in tantra. When we speak of trust in the tantric sense, we mean the actual experience of trusting in ourselves. There is a sense of genuine compassion towards ourselves, but without any self-indulgence. We are gentle and straightforward, but we are no longer playing the game of idiot compassion, using false kindness to protect ourselves unnecessarily. We also are completely free of spiritual materialism. There is a sense of one-hundred percent fresh air: things are clear and there is circulation, freshness, and understanding in our system. Our life feels quite okay. There is nothing to worry about, nothing to be that concerned about. That does not mean that all our problems have been solved and that everything is milk and honey. There is still a sense of struggle, but it has become very healthy. It is a learning process, a working process. In fact, struggle becomes the fuel for the bright burning flames of our energy.

When we have that attitude of trust, we can go further with the discipline of tantra and enter the samaya, or sacred bondage, of receiving abhisheka. When trust has been established as the working basis between student and teacher, mutual understanding and mutual openness take place constantly. There is openness to the tradition that exists, to the lineage, to ourselves, to our fellow students, and to our root guru—the actual performer of the abhisheka. The root guru is our vajra master, and he is the person who actually initiates us and gives us the abhisheka. So once we have that basic background of trust and openness, and once we have prepared ourselves properly, then we can receive abhisheka.

There are several divisions or levels of transmission that are part of an abhisheka. Each level is itself called an abhisheka, because it is a particular empowerment or transmission. Here we will discuss the first level, the first abhisheka, the abhisheka of form, which is a process of thoroughly training the student so that he is prepared and can enter the magic circle or mandala of the abhisheka properly. The abhisheka of form is a process of bringing the student up, raising him or her from the level of an infant to a king or queen. We will discuss this process in detail a little further on.

Traditionally, in medieval India and Tibet, the date for an abhisheka was set six months in advance. In that way students would have six months to prepare. Later the tantric tradition became extremely available, and some of the teachers in Tibet dropped that six-month rule—which seems to have been a big mistake. If we do not have enough time to prepare ourselves for an abhisheka, then the message doesn't come across. There is no real experience. That suspense—knowing that we are just about to receive an abhisheka but that, at the same time, we are suspended for six months—is extremely important. We have no idea what we are going to do. The text of the abhisheka may have already been presented to us, but still we have no idea what we are going to experience. In the meantime, we have six months to study how to handle ourselves and how to relate with the experience of abhisheka, which is described and explained in minute detail in the text.

The number of people who are going to receive a particular abhisheka is also very important. A certain chemistry takes place within a group of individuals and between certain types of people. Maybe twenty or twenty-five students should receive abhisheka, or maybe only three. It is at the discretion of the vajra master to decide on the number of students and to choose the particular students to be initiated, because he knows the students' development and their understanding. Receiving abhisheka is an extremely precious event. And the psychology that happens between the people involved and the environment that such people create together are right at the heart of the matter.

Receiving abhisheka is not the same as collecting coins or stamps or the signatures of famous people. Receiving hundreds and hundreds of abhishekas and constantly collecting blessing after blessing as some kind of self-confirmation has at times become a fad, a popular thing to do. This was true in Tibet in the nineteenth century as well as more recently in the West. That attitude, which reflects the recent corruption in the presentation of vajrayana, has created an enormous misunderstanding. People who collect successive abhishekas in this manner regard them purely as a source of identity and as a further reference point. They collect abhishekas out of a need for security, which is a big problem.

Jamgön Kongtrül the Great, a Tibetan teacher who lived in the nineteenth century, was raised and educated as an enlightened student of vajrayana. Because he received so many transmissions, it might seem that he was doing the same thing—collecting abhishekas.

But in his case it was an entirely different process because he felt, he experienced, and he understood what he studied. After he finished his basic training, he studied under and received all the teachings from more than one hundred and thirty-five teachers. Then he initiated a reformation of Buddhism in Tibet, which he called the Rime school. The term *Rime* literally means "without bias," an "ecumenical approach." The Rime school brought together the various contemplative traditions of Tibetan Buddhism to create a powerful practicing lineage, which we ourselves belong to. My predecessor, the tenth Trungpa tulku, also belonged to that lineage.

The Rime school made an enormous impression. For one thing, it generated a great deal of sarcasm and jealousy on the part of some practitioners: "Why make a big deal out of nothing? Why can't we just go on as we were and continue to buy abhishekas? What's wrong with what we are doing?" But Jamgön Kongtrül had seen that something was wrong with the tradition and practice; something was wrong with receiving a succession of abhishekas purely as collectors' items. He pointed out that problem by saying that if we have no understanding of the practicing lineage then we are just collecting piles of manure, and there is no point in that. A pile of manure may be ripe, smelly, and fantastic, but it is still a pile of shit. If we were manure experts, we could utilize it. But when we are actually collecting such manure to try to make it into food, that is out of the question.

This kind of spiritual materialism was present in Tibet from the nineteenth century onwards. Tibet had lost its communication with the outside world and was no longer hosting great teachers from other countries. It had become just a little plateau, a little island that had to survive by itself. Consequently, it became too inbred. In that atmosphere spiritual materialism began to develop. Abbots and great teachers were more concerned with building solid gold roofs on their temples, constructing gigantic Buddha images, and making their temples beautiful and impressive than with the actual practice of their lineage. They sat less and they did more business.

That was the turning point of Buddhism in Tibet. Tibet began to lose its connection with dharma and it slowly, very irritatingly and horrifically, began to turn into ugly spiritual materialism. Jamgön

Kongtrül the Great was like a jewel in a pile of manure. His wisdom was shining. He saw that it was necessary to call upon the eight great traditions of Buddhism in Tibet—which included the Gelug tradition, the Sakya tradition, the Kagyü tradition, and the Nyingma tradition—and bring them together: "Let us unite; let us work together within this contemplative tradition. Let us experience this tradition for ourselves, instead of inviting hundreds of artists to build glorious shrines. Let us experience how it feels to sit on our meditation cushions and do nothing." This reintroduction of practice, which had long been forgotten, was the focus of the contemplative reformation of Tibetan Buddhism during the nineteenth century.

As part of his effort to revitalize the contemplative tradition and bring together practice and experience, Jamgön Kongtrül compiled and edited many collections of the sacred teachings of the Practice Lineage of Buddhism in Tibet. One of these works is entitled *Dam Ngak Dzö*, which literally means "The Treasury of Oral Instructions." In it he describes how a person can properly experience abhisheka. In this commentary he also describes how tantric students should be treated in such a ceremony of empowerment. It is not purely that the ritual and ceremony should inspire awe in the students. In fact, they may be awed simply because they have no idea how to behave, how to handle themselves, or how to handle their state of mind in that situation. Consequently they become bewildered and feel overwhelmed. Jamgön Kongtrül explains that this mixture of inadequacy and awe is not the experience of the meeting of two minds.

You cannot take advantage of students if they do not know how to deal with the ceremony. When students feel freaked out, they have no handle or stepping stone, so they should be treated gently, freely, and kindly. They should have some understanding of the steps in the process they are about to go through: "This ceremony has such and such levels. First you relate with this, and then you can go on to the next level." Students should be guided as a mother raises her infant. She starts out by nursing her child, then she feeds him milk from a cow, then she feeds him broth, and finally she begins to introduce solid food. When the infant has been raised into a proper child, he knows how to drink liquid and how to chew and swallow meat. He even knows how to drink soup and eat vegetables at the same time.

Initiating tantric students in an abhisheka is precisely the same process. At the beginning of the ceremony the students are not capable of doing anything; they simply experience oneness. They are like infants who have not yet learned to drink cow's milk instead of their own mother's milk. Then the students begin to realize that their openness allows them to relate to the world and to emotions. At that stage they are fascinated by the ceremony and fascinated by the tantric tradition altogether. Finally, the students begin to feel that they are actually grasping the teachings and that the teachings make sense. They mean something personally, experientially. The students then can relate with the principles of the five buddha families. At that point in the abhisheka, the teacher presents, or confers, what are known as the five abhishekas of form, which are directly related to the five buddha families. Each one is an empowerment, and together they make up the first abhisheka.

This presentation of the first abhisheka is based on the tradition of anuttara yoga, which is the pinnacle of the three lower tantric yanas. According to the tradition of anuttara yoga, the first abhisheka of form is the abhisheka of the jar or vase. Actually, this abhisheka is symbolic of bathing. According to the custom in medieval India, when a person wanted to bathe himself, he would go out into a river with a jar, scoop up a jarful of water, and pour it over himself. So the jar abhisheka is a process of purifying. We are cleaning out the hidden corners of the body, seeing that our ears are clean and our armpits are clean. Any hidden corners in our basic make-up have to be cleansed.

In this case, the purification is obviously psychological. Psychologically we have smelly armpits that generate lots of odor for our neighbors and ourselves. We begin to dislike that psychological odor, and our neighbors might begin to dislike it as well. In fact, we feel completely revolted, which is a very positive step at this point because we actually have the means to clean up properly.

You may remember that the word abhisheka literally means "anointment." Through the vase abhisheka, we are cleaned out completely. It is similar to the Christian tradition of baptism or

christening, which also makes use of water as a symbol of psychologically cleansing oneself. The vase abhisheka is also like washing our
hands before we eat. If we go to the bathroom just before we have
lunch, we wash our hands. That is a basic and sensible law of human
conduct: we should taste our food rather than our excrement when
we eat. The vase abhisheka is the same kind of sensible approach. It
is connected with the vajra family. Water is a symbol of the sharpness and the clarity of vajra, which cleanses us of any psychological
dirt. Then, when we are cleaned out and fundamentally purified, we
can put on our clean clothes.

In an abhisheka, the students are regarded as princesses and
princes who are coming to court. They are just about to sit on the
throne and relate with their subjects, that is, with their subconscious gossip, their mind, their samsaric world. So the idea of
abhisheka is receiving royal treatment. The Tibetan word for abhisheka
is *wang (dbang)*, which simply means "empowerment." The student is
empowered as the royal ruler, the majestic one.

Before he gives an audience to the public, a king first bathes
and puts on his clothes. Then he puts on his crown. That is the
second abhisheka, the crown or coronation abhisheka. In this
abhisheka, the student is presented with a crown which has five
prongs and is inlaid with jewels. Each prong represents a different
buddha family: vajra, ratna, padma, karma, and buddha. Finally we
are coronated: we are made into a tantric master, or at least a
confident practitioner, a confident person. The crown abhisheka is
connected with the ratna family. There is a sense of being enriched
and a sense of plentifulness, lack of threat, openness, and generosity.

At this point in the abhisheka we are like a young king who is
very ambitious and youthful, but still does not know how to handle
his subjects. Although we have been coronated, our hands are just
resting in our lap and we have nothing to hold onto. In that condi-
tion we could feel quite self-conscious: there is a big crown sitting
on our head and we are dressed up in robes but our hands are just
loose. We could pick our nose or scratch our chin, but we still feel
awkward. At this point we are presented with the third abhisheka,
the abhisheka of the vajra. The idea is to give a royal toy to this little
prince or princess. The first toy we receive, which should be given

to us in the right hand, is the vajra scepter, or dorje, which we discussed earlier as the symbol of indestructibility. It represents immense power. Seven qualities characterize the vajra: it cannot be cut, it cannot be disintegrated, it cannot be obstructed, it is penetrating, it is fearless, it is open, and it is utterly destructive. According to tradition, the vajra is a weapon as well as a scepter. Each time the king throws the vajra, it goes out, it fulfills its deadly purpose, and it comes back into his hand.

The abhisheka of the vajra is related to the padma family. Padma here is the sense of being a beautiful lover. In this abhisheka you are acknowledged as a powerful person and at the same time you are told that you can make love without destroying somebody else. Rather, you could create by making love. So holding the vajra brings a feeling of compassion, warmth, and hospitality.

In the next abhisheka, the abhisheka of the bell, not only does the student have a scepter in the right hand, but as a royal personage, he or she also receives a musical instrument, a bell, in the left hand. The musical instrument signifies that we are not only concerned with our own compassion, our own crown, or our own cleanliness, but we have something to say. Rather than playing by ourselves with all our toys, we have something to proclaim. The bell, or *ghanta* in Sanskrit, is a karma family symbol, and this abhisheka is connected with karma family. Karma is the fulfillment of action. Here, it is the utterance of sound which cannot be blocked, sound which can be heard by anybody anywhere. If we are around the corner we can hear it; if we are far away we can hear it; if we are close by we can hear it. The karma sound of this bell is unobstructed: we cannot hide underneath our chair pretending we did not hear anything. The bell is heard and understood completely and thoroughly. It pierces our ears. The sound of this bell is also very high-pitched, which invokes wakefulness: we cannot fall asleep anymore, because the sound of the bell is too penetrating to our ears.

The fifth abhisheka also uses the vajra and bell, but in this abhisheka the bell and the vajra are fastened together at right angles with a silk ribbon. The king already has a clean body and beautiful clothes; he has a crown; he holds a scepter as a sign of power; and he has a bell for proclaiming—so what is lacking? He does not have a

name. We do not yet know which king we are. Who are we? That is
a problem: if we do not know who we are we have very little to say.
We may try to say something, but we have no idea what our name is
or what our status is—whether we are literate or illiterate, or even
whether we are actually a human being.

The first thing we usually say to people is, "How do you do?"
which is like ringing the bell. Then we introduce ourselves: "My name
is Jack Parsons, Julie Smith, or whatever." Similarly, in this abhisheka
we introduce ourselves to the world. So this abhisheka is called the
abhisheka of name. In this abhisheka our vajra master rings the bell
with the vajra attached to it above our heads, and at the same time as
the bell is rung, we are given a tantric name, which is traditionally
known as our secret name. This name is not publicized as is our
ordinary name, but when we need to use our power or to wake
someone up, we say our vajra name, our tantric name. The name
abhisheka is connected with the buddha family. It is the sense of
complete spaciousness and openness that comes when we finally,
thoroughly take our place in the vajra mandala.

These five abhishekas make up the abhisheka of form, which is
the first of four levels of transmission that traditionally make up the
complete ceremony of empowerment in anuttara yoga. When we
have received the abhisheka of form, there is a sense of enormous
psychological progress and psychological change. We have gone
through a whole process of being accepted and acknowledged: we
have our scepter, we can proclaim, and now we know our name as
well. We actually become a ruler of some kind.

A problem with many religious traditions is that they make a
point of condemning us. They talk about how wicked we are or how
terrible we are and how we have to pull ourselves together. And if
we do so, they promise us some candy or reward. But the vajrayana
is an entirely different approach. The tantric tradition builds us up so
we do not have to relate at the level of a donkey reaching for a carrot
anymore. The donkey has the carrot already, so the donkey should
feel good.

The basic point of abhisheka is not to zap us with magical power
but to bring us up slowly and gently so that we can experience
and relate with ourselves simply. Because we exist and we have

a body, therefore we can bathe ourselves. Having bathed, we can put our clothes on. Having dressed, we can put on our crown. Then we have something to hold in our hand and something to say. We can make a statement about why we are doing all this. And we have a name as well. This is the basic process of graduating from the ordinary world into the world of continuity, the tantric world. We finally become a real person. That is the basic meaning of abhisheka.

The ceremony of abhisheka is actually based on the example of the Buddha. It is said that Shakyamuni Buddha was once invited by King Indrabhuti to teach the dharma. The king said, "I would like to relate with my sense perceptions and my emotions. Could you give me some teachings so that I can work with them?" The Buddha said, "Oh, you want to hear tantra." And the king said, "Yes." Then the Buddha replied, "If that is the case, let me excuse my arhats and my hinayana and mahayana disciples from the room." So he asked his disciples to leave. Then the Buddha appeared to the king in royal costume and taught the first tantra, the *Guhyasamaja*. That was the first presentation of tantra.

So the Buddha is seen in different ways at different levels of practice. Unlike hinayana and mahayana, at the vajrayana level the Buddha is dressed as a king: he has a crown, he has a scepter in his hand, he has a royal gaze, and he behaves like a king. This is quite a different approach than the traditional hinayana or mahayana view. In fact, the vajrayana approach could be quite shocking to practitioners of the lower yanas. That is why the Buddha excused all his other disciples from the room before he introduced the tantric teachings.

Abhisheka, or empowerment, plays an extremely important part in tantric literature, tantric ceremony, and the tantric tradition altogether. One of the reasons that tantra is so rich is because it actually relates with human experience as a physical situation rather than as a lofty idea. In the hinayana we are struggling to maintain our awareness, and in the mahayana we are trying to be kind to our neighbors. Vajrayana Buddhism respects those disciplines, but it also transcends them and becomes the greatest idea of all.

Vajrayana deals much more directly with ego than the previous two yanas. In the abhisheka of form, we actually bathe ego, coronate ego, and give ego a scepter. Finally, when ego finds itself with everything it wants, it begins to flop. It begins to be so embarrassed that it becomes nonexistent. Then we can begin to build a new kingdom of egolessness. That is the tantric way. Sometimes I wonder who thought up tantra. It constantly amazes me. But it happened; it exists. Somebody actually thought up such an idea and transmitted it to people—and it actually works. It is very amazing. I suppose we could call it magic.

In going through the landscape of the tantric tradition, I have been very careful not to introduce the juicy tidbits at the beginning. I am being very faithful and orthodox and presenting the tradition in the same way that it was presented to me. To begin with, we need panic. We need that sense of nervousness or uncertainty. It is absolutely necessary. And then, having gone through such a period already, we arrive at the point at which we are capable of receiving abhisheka. Then we are much more at home, and we are complimented by our teacher and our world. I experienced this myself in my training in Tibet.

In my education, I was constantly criticized. If I leaned back I was criticized and told that I should sit up. I was told that I should always make pleasant conversation with visiting dignitaries and that I should be hospitable to them. At that level, the training was very simple and not particularly tantric. Every time I did something right—or I thought I was doing something right—I was criticized even more heavily. I was cut down constantly by my tutor. He slept in the corridor outside my door, so I could not even get out. He was always there, always watching me. He would be serving me and watching me at the same time. My other teachers would all work through him so that they themselves did not have to put embarrassing pressure on me. Instead, they could pressure my tutor, and in turn my tutor would pressure me—which I thought was very clever. It was also very claustrophobic and somewhat painful.

I was constantly cut down. I had been brought up strictly since infancy, from the age of eighteen months, so that I had no other reference point such as the idea of freedom or being loose. I had no idea what it was like to be an ordinary child playing in the dirt or playing with toys or chewing on rusted metal or whatever. Since I did not have any other reference point, I thought that was just the way the world was. I felt somewhat at home, but at the same time I felt extraordinarily hassled and claustrophobic. It did not feel so good.

At the same time I knew that there were little breaks, like going to the bathroom—which was an enormous relief. The only time I was not being watched was when I went to the bathroom. It was my one free time. Usually I would feel an enormous rush of fresh air, because bathrooms were built overhanging cliffs and had big holes in the floor. I would feel the fresh air coming up, and at the same time I would know that nobody was watching me, telling me how to defecate properly. Apart from that, I was always watched. Even when I ate, I was watched and told how to eat properly, how to extend my arm, how to watch the cup, how to bring it to my mouth. If I made a big noise while swallowing, I was criticized for eating "crocodile style." I was told that rinpoches, or other important tulkus, were not supposed to swallow crocodile style. Everything was very personal from that point of view—to say the least.

Then, very interestingly, I stopped struggling with the authorities, so to speak, and began to develop. I just went on and on and on. Finally that whole world began to become my reference point rather than being a hassle—although the world was full of hassles. At that point, my tutor seemed to become afraid of me; he began to say less. And my teachers began to teach me less because I was asking them too many questions. I was interested in what they had to say and I pursued them for more and more, so that they began to have a more relaxed approach than even I wanted.

My tutor was frightened because he did not know exactly how to handle me. I thought that maybe this was all some kind of joke, and that my teachers would leave me alone for ten days and then catch me again. But ten days went by, and a month went by, and finally six months—and nothing changed. The situation just went on and on. Something was actually working. Something was finally beginning to click. The discipline had become part of my system. My tutors and my teachers were pushed by me instead of my being pushed by them. I wanted to know more and more about what was happening, and they began to run out of answers. They were hassled by me because I was so wholehearted. They became afraid that they could not keep up with me anymore.

I'm telling you this because there are parallels between my own experience and that of other tantra students. It is a question of interest. Once you are really into something, you become part of that experience, or it becomes part of you. When you become part of the teachings, you are no longer hassled. You are no longer an entity separate from the teachings. You are an embodiment of them. That is the basic point.

CHAPTER ELEVEN

Being and Manifesting

The tantric approach is not mystical experience alone, but it is concerned with how we can perceive reality in a simple and direct way. In our normal confused, or samsaric, way of perceiving and handling the world, we perceive reality on the level of body, on the level of emotions, and on the level of mindlessness, which is traditionally known as basic ignorance. Body refers to basic self-consciousness, which includes the various sense perceptions: thought, vision, sound, taste, touch, and smell. Emotion includes aggression, passion, ignorance, jealousy, pride, and all other emotions and feelings. Mindlessness, or basic ignorance, refers to a state of total bewilderment: fundamentally we have no idea what we are doing or what we are experiencing, and we are completely missing the point all the time. Those three major principles—body, emotions, and mindlessness—are how we experience our life.

By "body," to begin with, we mean an actual physical body. Bodies may be well-shaped, fat or thin, functional or nonfunctional. Some bodies see but cannot hear. Some bodies hear but cannot see. Some bodies feel but cannot see or hear. Some bodies hear and see but cannot feel, and some bodies can do the whole thing. There are all kinds of bodies, and there are all kinds of physical experiences, depending on whether we are lame or deaf or dumb or completely healthy. Still, we all have the same basic experience, that is, the experience of the body, the experience of reality at that very simple level.

In the *sutras*, the Buddhist scriptures, Buddha once said to Ananda: "Ananda, if there is no body, there is no dharma. If there is no food, there is no dharma. If there are no clothes, there is no dharma. Take care of your body, for the sake of the dharma." Relating with the body is extremely important in the tantric tradition. However, we don't make a personal "trip" out of it. We could become a vegetarian and sneer at meat eaters. We could wear pure cotton clothing and renounce wearing any leather. Or we could decide to search for a country to live in that is free from pollution. But any of those approaches could be going too far. When someone becomes a vegetarian, he stops eating meat, but he still might take a bloodthirsty delight in peeling bananas and crunching his teeth into peaches and cooking eggplants as meat substitutes. So our attempts to relate with the body can become very complicated.

I'm not particularly advocating eating meat or otherwise at this point. Rather, I am pointing out that we do not accept our body as it is, and we do not accept our world. We are always searching for some way to have an easy ride. When we feel unhappy or uncomfortable, we think that we would like to go somewhere else, up or down or wherever. Some people call it hell, some people call it heaven, but whatever it is, we would like to have an easy ride somewhere.

It is actually quite humorous how we view the cosmos, our world. We view it as if it were not a real world at all, but a world we could control. Sometimes we treat the world as a problem child who is trying to suggest all kinds of evil things to us. Sometimes we treat our world as a priest or master who is telling us that everything is good, that whatever we do is fine: there are flowers, there are meadows, there is wildlife, and the world is a fantastic place. But fundamentally, we haven't really made up our mind what this world is all about. Sometimes we think we have, but there is still a flicker of doubt. Whenever a temptation comes up, we regard it as fantastically evil or challenging and we jump sideways, like a tempermental horse. There is a big problem with that: we have not accepted our world thoroughly, properly, and fully.

The world we are talking about is a very simple world, an extremely simple world which is made out of concrete, plastic, wood, stones, greenery, pollution, and thin air. Actually, every one of us is sitting or standing on that world. Shall we say this is the real world or should we pretend that the world is something else? You and I are both here. If we feel guilty, it's too late. This is our world, here, right now. We could say, "Hey, that's not true. I can go out in my car and drive up in the mountains. I can camp out in the mountains in my sleeping bag." But sleeping in our sleeping bag is the same as sitting on a rug or carpet. Somehow we cannot get away from the world. This world is the real world, the actual world, the world we experience, the world in which we are thriving. This is the world that communicates to our sense perceptions. We can smell incense or tobacco or food cooking; we can see and hear what is around us. This is our world.

Wherever we are, we carry this world with us. If we go out to a lecture, we see the stage, the backdrop, the podium, the speaker; we smell the musty air in the hall; and we hear the seat creaking under us. When we go home, we take this world with us. We look back again and again, remembering where we have been, so we can't get away from this world. By the time we look back, of course, "this world" has become "that world," which is the world of the past. But our memory is still of this world, nevertheless. Otherwise we could not have a memory. So we are still in this world, this real world made out of thisness, in fact, made out of us. If somebody asks what this world is made out of, what the substance of it is, it is 75% "I" and 25% "am." So this is our world: "I am" is our world, and we can not get away from it.

The next level is the world of emotions. It is not exactly a different world, but it is a different perspective, seeing things from a different angle. There are many ways that emotions color our experience. When we are depressed and angry, we begin to feel a grudge and to grind our teeth. We find our world fantastically aggressive: everything is irritating, including fence posts in the countryside that have harmlessly placed themselves there with barbed wire or electric wire going across them. We feel that we have been invaded, raped. We feel so bad about this world.

When we experience aggression we feel that everything is an expression of injustice. There is too much concrete, too much steel, too much grease, too much pollution, and we feel very angry and frustrated. We are so involved with this world of emotions that, although we might have a beautiful sunny day, fantastic weather, and a fantastic view, we still grind our teeth. We feel that the world is trying to mock us. The clear blue sky is trying to mock us or insult us. The beautiful sunshine is embarrassing to look at, and the fantastic full moon and the beautiful clouds around it are an insult. There is constant hate, enormous hate, so much so that it is almost unreal. We feel that we are actually levitating off the ground because we are so angry. We feel that our feet are not attached to the ground, that we are hovering above the world, because there is such a sense of aggression taking place.

On the other hand, if we are passionate, if we are in love or in a lustful state, we begin to feel that there is an enormous amount of glue sprayed all over the world that is trying to stick to us. Our only frustration is that we do not have enough money to buy all the beautiful clothes we see in shop windows, all the beautiful antiques we see in the shops, and all the beautiful food or wealth that exists. We may try to project an image of aloofness or specialness: "I'm not going to be like the rest of my countrymen. When I buy clothes, I'm going to buy special ones, not like the rednecks." But that is just a sidetrack. Fundamentally, the juice of the juice is that we *want* so much, and we begin to spray our own glue all over things. We want to be stuck to things, to persons, objects, wealth, money, parents, relatives, friends, or whatever. So we begin to spray this crude glue all over the place. We are asking to be stuck.

Hopefully, we think, we can pull things or people back into our territory: "Once I get stuck to something, I've got enough sanity and enough power to pull it back to me. I want to make sure, to begin with, that my glue is strong enough. Then when I am stuck to my friend, I can step back, and my friend will be so stuck to me that I will not have to worry. He or she is always going to be with me, because my glue is so powerful, so strong, and so tough." That is the game we play. But the problem is that things get turned around, and we find ourselves stuck. The ground we create is too solid, too powerful, and we cannot step back. Then we might scream and begin to worry. But that panic connected with passion is another matter altogether, beyond the subject we are discussing at this point.

Another emotional style is called stupidity or ignorance. It occurs when we are so absorbed in our world that we miss the sharp points. For example, if somebody is yelling at us, calling our name, we might answer him and we might not. We want to shield ourselves from the world. The world makes us blush, and we begin to hide behind a timid smile. If somebody insults us, we try to walk away. We are trying to save face by ignoring reality. If somebody is irritating us, we feel we can't be bothered: "Let's change the subject. Let's talk about something else—my fantastic trip to Peru. I took photographs there when I was with the Indians. It was fantastic!" We become very skillful at changing the subject of conversation. Sometimes we shield ourselves with a little sense of humor, but the humor is usually somewhat superficial. Fundamentally we are ignoring the situation. The sharp edges that come up are pushed away or ignored. We play deaf and dumb.

There are many different emotions, but these three—aggression, passion, and ignorance—are the basic emotions or basic styles that make up the second level of perception.

The third level of perception is the ultimate idea of bewilderment or confusion. It is much more fundamental than the emotional style of ignorance that we just discussed. Basic bewilderment or mindlessness is experiencing things as if the world did not exist and we did not exist. We could almost view this level of perception as mystical experience because it is so solid and pervasive. It is like being entranced by the shimmering reflection of light on a pond: there is a sense of being stunned, fixed solid—so fixed that the experience is no longer experience, but fixation. That kind of frozen experience is extremely confusing, but nevertheless, we do not want to let go of our fixation; we do not want to let go of the phenomenal world. We would like to hang onto it, to keep ourselves attached to the world, as though we had tentacles with suction cups on the ends.

We are determined to ignore the possibility of any spaciousness in our experience. This level of bewilderment is the fundamental style of ego. Space is completely frozen into mindlessness. In such a state, it is impossible to step out or to step in. There is a sense of being fixed, being part of a rock or a mountain. It is like flat air, which doesn't have any energy. We begin to feel that our head is being flattened on top, as though we were wearing a cast iron frying pan on our head. Our head is stuck to that pan, and we are constantly carrying that big flat metal object on our head. Our head is not even stuck to a sheet of corrogated iron—that texture would be too interesting. This is completely flat. We do not feel exactly squashed, but we feel that we are being weighted down by the force of gravity.

This kind of heavy-handed mindlessness makes us feel that we shouldn't worry about anything at all. On the one hand, everything is there and at the same time it is confusingly not there. We can't be bothered to talk about anything at all. We are carrying a cast iron head, our shoulders are stiff, our neck is stiff, and in fact, our whole body is made out of cast iron. Since our legs are cast iron, we can't even move. But we still have a heartbeat, which is a reference point. The only things functioning are our lungs and heart. We breathe in and out and our heart beats: that is the ultimate level of stupidity or bewilderment.

We have been discussing the samsaric way of handling our world, in terms of the three levels of samsaric perception: body, emotions, and mindlessness. There is a definite tantric approach to those three levels of perception, which is known as the principle of the three *kayas*, or the *trikaya*. *Kaya* is a Sanskrit word that simply means "body." There is a correspondence between the three levels we have discussed and the three kayas. In the language of tantra, the level of body corresponds to the kaya or body of manifestation, the *nirmanakaya*. The level of emotions corresponds to the body of complete joy, the *sambhogakaya*, and the level of bewilderment or ignorance corresponds to total space, the *dharmakaya*. There is no tension or contradiction between the samsaric and the tantric descriptions. Rather the tantric principle of the three kayas shows how we could relate to the levels of body, emotions, and bewilderment that already exist within our state of being.

Traditionally, dharmakaya is the first kaya, corresponding to the samsaric level of mindlessness. *Dharma* means "law," "norm," or "truth," among other definitions. The teachings of the Buddha are called the dharma, the truth. The first kaya is called *dharmakaya*, the "body of truth," because the dharma speaks completely and totally in accordance with the language of ignorant people. The starting point for hearing the dharma is confusion. If we are not ignorant and confused—thoroughly, utterly, and completely—then there is no dharma. At the same time, dharma speaks the language of intelligence, which is the opposite of ignorance. The dharma is able to communicate the truth by relating to the confusion of sentient beings.

Dharmakaya is the original state of being, which transcends our basic state of mindlessness. It is the opposite of having a cast iron pan on our head. It is a state of complete freedom. It is so free that the question of freedom does not even apply. It is complete and it is open—thoroughly open, utterly open, magnificently open. Dharmakaya is so completely open that the question of openness does not apply anymore at all, and so completely spacious that reference points do not make any difference.

The second kaya is the level of emotional manifestation. This is called *sambhogakaya*, which literally means "body of joy." The dharmakaya, as we have discussed, is completely open and completely free. At the level of sambhogakaya we are looking at the emotions that are manufactured or manifested out of that. The emotions that manifest out of this state of openness transcend the samsaric emotions, including aggression, passion, and ignorance. In the sambhogakaya, emotions manifest as the transcendent or completely enlightened versions of the five buddha families that we discussed in chapter nine. When they manifest in this way, the emotions provide tremendous capability and enormous scope for relating with the universe. There is accommodation for dualism, for relating with this and that if necessary, because from this point of view duality is not particularly regarded as a threat or unkosher.

This accommodation provides tremendous freedom. There is a sense of celebration in which emotions are no longer a hassle.

The third kaya, the *nirmanakaya*, is the "body of emanation," the body of existence or manifestation. It is the manifestation of our mind and our body. It is also the manifestation of the bodies of those who have already experienced or gone through the other two kayas, and who then manifest on the third level, the nirmanakaya. In that sense the nirmanakaya refers specifically to the vajra master or teacher who is here on earth. Such a teacher has achieved the dharmakaya and the sambhogakaya, but in order to communicate with our body, our food, our clothes, and our earth—that is, with our sense perceptions—he needs a manifested body. It is necessary that the teacher manifest in the nirmanakaya in order to communicate with us and to teach the vajrayana and the entire buddhadharma.

In studying tantra, we relate with all three kayas simultaneously by relating to the vajra master, who embodies all three. The three kayas are not abstract principles, but we can relate to them experientially, personally, spiritually, and transcendently, all at the same time. As we develop to the level of the teacher's body, the level of nirmanakaya, then we begin to experience the sambhogakaya. At that level emotions are transmuted and are workable. Beyond that, we also begin to tune in to the dharmakaya, which is open, all-pervading space.

If we are going to study tantra, it is necessary to understand the trikaya principle of being and manifesting. In tantric practice the first step is to realize the level of body, the nirmanakaya. Then we see that the five buddha families are related with the sambhogakaya or the level of emotions. Beyond that it is necessary to transcend both the bodily and the emotional level, which is the dharmakaya, high above. When we discuss maha ati in the closing chapter, you may understand more about dharmakaya. But first it is necessary to understand the importance of relating with the body, or earthly existence, and relating with the vajra master, the great teacher who exists on earth. In some sense such a teacher is a magician, a conjurer: he has achieved total space, conquered the level of emotions, and he actually exists in an earthly body.

CHAPTER TWELVE

The Question of Magic

The Sanskrit word for magic is *siddhi*, which means actualizing or working with the energy that exists in the realm of experience and the realm of physical being. Unfortunately, in the Western world, the concept of magic seems to be associated with mysteriousness and impossible powers, such as turning fire into water or the floor into the sky. So magic is considered to be possible only for those few chosen people who develop mysterious magical powers. In comic books, for instance, magical things happen because a person possesses a certain power that he exercises over other people, either destroying them or helping them. Such a magician can change a giant into a dwarf, a mute into a bard, a cripple into a runner, and so forth.

In the West, we often treat spirituality with that comic book approach, and we view spiritual discipline as the process through which we will eventually end up as magicians. We feel that, although we may have a few little problems as beginners, when we become highly accomplished persons, we won't have these problems. We will be able to shake them off and do anything we want. That is the simpleminded concept of spiritual practice and the simpleminded concept of magic: that once we are accomplished persons we will be able to do anything. We will be able to shake the universe, to change the shape of fleas and the habits of mice, to turn tigers into cats and cats into tigers.

Genuine mystical experience, according to either the Judeo-Christian tradition or the Buddhist tradition, has nothing to do with that kind of mysteriousness. It is not that the mysteriousness finally manifests, and then we realize that spirituality has some value after all: "Now we don't need to ride elevators; we can just levitate." That is the ultimate idea of automation, the true American dream. From that point of view, the world is a nuisance; it is problematic; it gets in our way. So we hope we can change its course once we graduate to a higher level. Obviously, there is a problem with that approach to spirituality.

A deeper problem is that this approach is based on misunderstanding the world of ego. We think that ego can achieve enormous power beyond its present ability, which is called "magic." In that case, we do not have to give up anything at all. We can just latch on to some greater power and expend further energy in the direction of ego. That is an enormous problem, an enormous blockage, and that is precisely why it is necessary for potential students of tantra to go through a gradual process and to give up any idea of the rapid path. It is necessary to start slowly, very slowly, to start at the bottom and grow up slowly. In that way our simpleminded version of the cosmos or the universe changes and becomes more real, more personal, and more direct. Our world becomes workable; it no longer remains separate from our basic being at all. The world contains invitations for us to participate, and we in turn extend our invitation and willingness to participate to the world. In that way, the world can come into us and we can get into the world.

Beyond that, there *is* a magical aspect of the world. That magic does not have to be sought, but it happens by itself. It is not as sensational as we might expect. The greatest magic of all is to be able to control and work with ego, our mind. So we could say that magic begins at home, with our own minds. If we couldn't practice magic at home, we would be at a loss. We would have no place to begin. So magic begins at home.

We might ask: "What is so magical about all this? We have been working with ego all along, throughout our Buddhist training. What is so special about this magic?" We don't see anything particularly extraordinary about it. That is true. It is quite ordinary. In fact, the ordinary aspect becomes so powerful that it *is* magic. If something is extraordinary, it is usually a mechanical invention, something sensational but feeble. But because of ordinariness, magic is possible.

As far as tantra is concerned, magic is relating with the world on as ordinary a level as possible: we make flowers grow; we make the sun rise and the moon set. If we stay up long enough we will see the moon set and the sun rise. If we would like to watch the sun rise, we have to stay up so late that it finally becomes early. There is some discipline involved with that. We can't give up and go to bed to take a rest. If we do, quite possibly we will miss the sunrise.

The question of magic at this point is completely relevant to our life, to our path, to our actual practice. Magic is very real, direct and personal. It is so personal that it becomes excruciating. It is at the level of excruciation that we have a glimpse of magic. We find ourselves on a threshold, and at that point, we can, in fact, push ourselves one step further. That threshold occurs when we think we have gone too far in extending ourselves to the world. There is some kind of warning, and at the same time a faint invitation takes place. Quite possibly, we chicken out at that point because it requires so much effort and energy to go further. We feel we have put in enough effort and energy already, and we don't want to go beyond that. So-called sensible people wouldn't take such a risk: "Oh no! We have gone far enough; we mustn't go too far. Let's step back."

According to the *Tibetan Book of the Dead*, when a brilliant light comes to us in the pardo, or after-death state, we shy away from it. When a pleasant, faint, soothing light comes to us, we go towards it. In choosing the dimmer light we come back to square one, which is samsara. The point at which we can either extend ourselves further and go towards an unfamiliar brilliance, or return to a more soothing and familiar dimness is the threshold of magic. It is very personal. We feel pushed, hassled, and exposed through our practice. All kinds of irritations and all kinds of boundaries begin to come up, and we would like to stay within our territory, within those boundaries. We don't really want to step beyond them. We fear that in stepping beyond those boundaries we might do something beyond the boundaries of the teachings, something beyond the level of basic human sanity. Basically, we fear that we might destroy ourselves if we go beyond the territory of survival.

Such boundaries or thresholds always come up, and we really do not want to push anymore. But some kind of push is necessary. We might say, "Well, we have given our income and our possessions to the church. We have committed ourselves. We have signed our names on the dotted line. We pay our dues. We subscribe to your magazine. We do everything." But there is still something left behind. We are still missing the point. Those commitments are very easy to make. At this point, it is a question of giving up our arms and our legs. Even that might be easy to do. We can give up our hair, we can give up our beard, we can take off our clothes. But we have no idea, none whatsoever, how to give up our heart and brain.

Once we give up our heart and brain, the magic begins. It actually does. That is the spark. We give up our little heart, our little brain, and then we get greater nothingness. That is where the magic begins. We do not get anything back in return, as such, because we actually have given up; but still something happens. Actual magic begins there. The magic cannot begin unless we are willing to step over the threshold. We have to step on the electric fence that has been keeping us inside the corral, and then we have to step over it. We might get a mild shock or a violent shock in the process, but that is absolutely necessary. Otherwise there is no tantra; there is no magic.

According to the tantric tradition, there are four levels of magic. The first is *one-pointedness*. In this case, we are not talking about one-pointedness as it is often described in hinayana meditation practice. We are not talking about a highly sharpened, pointed needle that pierces through discursive mind, enabling us to develop our mindfulness. The vajrayana version of mindfulness or one-pointedness is like a dull needle, a dagger made out of stone rather than efficient stainless steel. When we sew fabric with a sharp needle, the needle sews through the texture of the fabric without damaging it. The needle just goes in and out, and consequently our clothes are made very efficiently with almost invisible seams. In vajrayana one-pointedness, we are not only going through the web of the fabric, but we are crushing what is there. When we crush the fabric, there is no obstacle. It is thorough penetration, very, very personal and very real.

So one-pointedness, or the first level of magic, is a particular kind of penetration. Wherever there are obstacles, they are acknowledged, and then they are cut through very bluntly. Therefore there is a hole, a gate, or an entrance point. A sharp needle is sneaky and efficient and keeps apologizing to each strand of fabric, making each one feel better. With such a needle, one piece of fabric can be joined to another quite beautifully, without destroying or damaging the fabric. It is a very polite approach. Tantric one-pointedness, on the other hand, is blunt and not at all polite. Emotions occur and are experienced; they are not suppressed in a neurotic fashion, but instead they are dealt with directly, in their own place.

The second level of magic is called *simplicity* or noncomplication. Literally, it is nonexaggeration. Usually we find ourselves exaggerating. This exaggeration takes the form of spiritual materialism, trying to acquire all kinds of spiritual techniques and disciplines, and it also takes the form of psychological materialism, or trying to acquire all kinds of little metaphysical theories and experiences. The point here is that, having already been penetrated by the vajrayana one-pointedness, the phenomenal world has been related with properly, fully and thoroughly. It can exist in its own way; therefore simplicity is there already. In this case, simplicity does not mean being a harmless person who lives in a hermitage and is so kind and good that he would not kill a flea. Simplicity is noncomplication rather than romantic simplicity. This means, again, that there is no need for further exaggeration.

Often, when we refer to somebody as simple, we mean that the person is slightly dumb or naive. He is so simple that he does not know how to be sophisticated or complicated. We might find that type of energy very refreshing, but such simplicity is regressing rather than progressing in any way. In this case, simplicity is self-existence. Something is simple because of its own magical qualities. For instance, fire burns by its own simplicity but still has its energy.

A rock has its magic because it sits still and never gets bored. A river keeps flowing in a simple way; it never gets bored and never gives up its course. So the qualities of self-existence are directness and simplicity, rather than purely being naive or good or kind.

The next level of magic is known as *one taste*. Because things have a self-existing simplicity, they do not need any reference point. That is one taste: no need for further reference point. It is direct, one flavor. Usually, sugar is sweet because salt is salty, but such reference points do not apply. One taste is a one-shot deal. If you feel extreme pain and frustration, you *feel* it. Often, I find students saying that they feel extremely pained and frustrated, but they cannot understand why. There is some element of truth in that. There may be magic in that, in fact. The students are not being analytical but direct. They feel the nowness of the pain—or of the pleasure—as it is, personally, directly, simply. That magic is very powerful, very important.

The fourth level of magic is known as *nonmeditation*. In this case, meditation is the idea of contemplating some object, such as visualizing a candle, a rose, or a clear pond. We find ourselves associating with what we have visualized: we become a living rose. When we have finished meditating on the rose, we begin to feel like a rose—rosy. But in nonmeditation, we do not meditate *on* anything. It is beyond reference point of subject and object. It is just simple, direct personal experience.

Nonmeditation provides a contrast to our expectations and constant sense of wanting. We always want something. We want to bring something in constantly, all the time. We want it badly, seemingly, but that is questionable. What is this wanting? "I would like a blah blah blah. Could I do blah blah blah blah?" We manifest our wanting in all kinds of ways, but it is all the same thing. "I want to eat. I don't even want to chew. Once I get food inside my mouth, I just want to swallow." The magical level of nonmeditation is entirely different from that constant wanting. Nonmeditation is not necessarily *not* wanting as such, or being dispassionate and cool and good. Rather, we are not particularly hungry. We are not particularly full either; nonetheless, we are not particularly hungry. We can accommodate food if something to eat comes up. It is welcome, even fantastic, but let us eat properly, in a nonmeditative way.

That is the greatest magic of all. At the final or fourth level of the magical process, we do not just perform magic because our magic wand works. When an angry soldier fires his machine gun at his enemies, each time the machine gun operates properly and kills his enemies, he licks his lips with enormous satisfaction. Somehow magic doesn't happen that way. Magic is an expression of total nonaggression and an expression of total energy and power at the same time.

The question at this point might be whether what we have discussed is magical enough. It feels slightly toned-down and too sensible. But at this point we haven't experienced those four levels of magic personally, so we have no idea how powerful they are. The little glimpse of energy we experience by studying tantra is perhaps one-hundredth of the tantric energy taking place—and even then we might experience it as too much. But there is more to come. There is a great deal more to come, indeed. The great Indian pandit Naropa once said that practicing tantra is like trying to ride a burning razor. Maybe he was right.

CHAPTER THIRTEEN

The Tantric Journey

Y_{ana} is a Sanskrit word that literally means "vehicle." The three major yanas or vehicles of practice are, as we know, hinayana, mahayana, and vajrayana. Then there are further subdivisions, or subtleties. There are six yanas within vajrayana: kriyayoga yana, upayoga yana, yoga yana, mahayoga yana, anuyoga yana, and maha ati. Before discussing any of the tantric yanas specifically, we need to examine the basic idea of yana or path in connection with the tantric idea of continuity.

From our earlier discussion we know that tantra means continuity or thread. The tantric notion of continuity is quite special. Continuity obviously cannot take place without some means to continue ourselves. So the question is, "Who is continuing? What is continuing?" When we become tantric practitioners, we have discussed and studied the hinayana and mahayana levels of Buddhism already, but we still do not know completely who or what is making the journey. According to the vajrayana, nobody is making the journey; but if there is no traveller, how is it possible to have a path? Of course there is the possibility that there is no path, no yana. But we cannot just *say* that there is no path. We have to

117

acknowledge the phenomenological-experiential level: we have to relate to our own experience rather than simply making metaphysical assumptions such as that path does not exist.

We have to come back to square one: "What is this? Who am I?" The simplest way to approach this question is by realizing that it does not really matter who asks the question, but we need to see whether the question *itself* exists or not. Where does the question come from? It seems to come from curiosity and fascination, wanting to find the original truth. But where does that curiosity come from? How is it possible for there to be a question at all? From the point of view of the questionless state of being, questions are only fabrications; and since the question does not exist, therefore the questioner does not exist either. We have to work backwards using this type of logic.

For instance, we say that since there is no sun, it must be nighttime. That is proper logic. We could say that it must be nighttime because it is dark, which in turn means that there is no sun, but that is weak logic. The questioning process has to work back to the first flash of reality. After that first flash of reality is experienced, *then* one begins to question reality and whether reality exists in its own right or not. In fact it doesn't, because reality depends on the perceiver of reality. Since such a perceiver does not exist, therefore reality itself does not exist either. We have to work with that kind of logic; otherwise our understanding becomes too linear, too theistic.

So the question of a perceiver and the question of being is purely a phantom of our experience, purely a phantom, and it is questionable whether this phantom exists or not. On the one hand, the phantom does exist because of its phantomlike quality; but on the other hand, the phantom does not exist, also because of its phantomlike quality. We are cutting our throat if we discuss it, as if we were swallowing a razor blade.

With that understanding of egolessness or nonexistence, we begin to develop what is known as the knowledge of egoless insight, *lhakthong dagme tokpe sherap (lhag-mthong bdag-med rtogs-pa'i shes-rab)*. *Lhakthong* means "insight," *dagme* means "egoless," *tokpe* means "realization," and *sherap* means "knowledge." Without that knowledge there is no way of understanding vajrayana or tantric experience at all. Egolessness may seem to you to be just another concept, but it is absolutely necessary.

A sense of nonexistence or egolessness is the essential background for understanding the difference between nontheistic and theistic traditions. In comparing theism and nontheism we are not arguing about the existence of God, but about whether the *perceiver* of God exists or not. Having understood very clearly and precisely that the perceiver does not exist, we therefore conclude that God does not exist either. In the tantric tradition continuity has nothing to do with divine providence, since the notion of divinity has already been discarded. The continuity of tantra is simply the sense of path or journey, which takes place constantly. This journey is by no means an illusion. It is a real journey, a journey that takes place on the planet Earth in this particular solar system, in this particular country, for that matter.

When we refer to a journey, it seems to be quite clear that we are not talking about struggle or ambition. On the other hand, maybe we *are* talking in terms of struggle and ambition: ambition in the sense that we are inspired into the nowness, this very moment; and struggle in that a sense of exertion or discipline in the practice is necessary. This seems to be a contradiction. On the one hand we are talking about nonbeing, no world, nonexistence; and on the other hand we are discussing the process of the path, how we could proceed along a path and exert ourselves. Isn't there a hole in our logic? If we split hairs in that way, there is no truth anywhere, none whatsoever. Let it just be that way; let us have contradictions.

At the same time, let us be suspicious of the nature of the path. That is great; that is precisely what is needed. We should not become so gullible that if we are asked to lick our teacher's bottom we are willing to do so. That becomes somewhat ugly and too gullible. It is good that we have questions in our mind, that we have such suspicion and such unyielding pride. Such suspicion is required for the study of tantra in particular, as well as for studying the rest of the Buddhist teachings. We are not asked to take anything at its word.

For the tantric practitioner the point is that a sense of journey takes place. Whether the journey is regarded as a hypothetical journey, a cynical journey, or an actual spiritual journey, some kind of journey is taking place continually, and we have to acknowledge it. It might seem that our own journey is a backward journey; we might feel that we started with a point of reference in which we had confidence but that now we find ourselves quite uncertain. Or we may be uncertain whether we are going forward or backward.

In tantra, it is necessary to have pride that we are taking a journey; it does not really matter whether it is a forward or a backward journey. A journey is actually taking place—that is what counts. It is like aging. We know that we are getting physically older all the time. We might find ourselves becoming infantile psychologically, but in that case, we are an old person being infantile rather than actually a baby. We know that we are getting physically older as long as we have a body. We are developing grey hair, we are becoming somewhat inaccurate in our physical behavior, our sight is becoming blurry, our speech is becoming slightly old-fashioned, our hearing system is degenerating slightly, and our taste in food and our interest in excitement or entertainment is becoming somewhat numb and dulled. We are getting old. Whether we regard that as going backward, becoming infantile, or going forward, approaching our death, something is happening to us. We could consider that process of aging as a metaphor for the spiritual journey. Whether we like it or not, we *are* moving forward.

When we become a Buddhist, we become a refugee: we take the refuge vow and commit ourselves to the Buddhist path. We make the preliminary decision to call ourselves Buddhists. After that we slowly begin to develop the confidence that we are not only working on ourselves but that we can also work with others. Then we take another vow, called the bodhisattva vow. As we proceed further, we are ready to take tantric transmission, or abhisheka. We are still making a journey. We might feel that we are going backward or forward—but that is simply the play of emotions. If we feel we are becoming infantile, we are learning; if we think we are an insignificant old man, we are still learning. A learning process takes place constantly, throughout the whole path.

It would be very difficult to go through each of the tantric yanas in detail since many of you are beginning practitioners. So I would like to take a more general approach in discussing the tantric journey. We could discuss the beginning, the middle, and the end of the path, that is, kriya yoga, the first yana; anuttara tantra, the culmination of the first three; and ati yana, the final yana. The main point is that the same psychological attitude permeates all the tantric yanas, the same continuity based on the nonexistence of ego. There is a continual sense of journey throughout the path. We have developed a sense of egolessness at the hinayana level, we have understood the compassionate activities that might take place at the mahayana level, and now we are approaching the vajrayana level. There is the continuity of an inspired student who is well disciplined, highly inspired by working with others, and who now is coming to grips with reality properly and thoroughly.

The first tantric yana is kriya yoga. *Kriya* literally means "action," so kriya yoga is the yoga of action. The basic approach of kriya yoga is that of purity or cleanliness, which in this case means understanding reality from the sharpest possible perspective, the clearest possible point of view. In order to see the vajra world or the tantric world properly, thoroughly and clearly, we have to see it in a highly purified way. Otherwise, rather than creating the clear vision of kriya yoga, we will begin to fixate on spots of dirt all over the place. Actions such as vegetarianism, taking baths frequently, and leading a very pure life are recommended in kriya yoga, but they are by no means "trips," because before we begin such actions we already have been trained. We already have been educated in the hinayana and mahayana. Therefore we are able to practice the disciplines of kriya yoga properly. We are not just presented with kriya yoga suddenly out of nowhere, as though our mother decided to wean us by abruptly taking away her nipples.

One of the basic notions of kriya yoga is that there is both purity and dirt in emotions. Initially, emotions occur in a spontaneous way. Then we interpret those spontaneous emotions to our own advantage. Having done so, we begin to possess our emotions as territory: we have our logic and our arguments, and other people's interpretations seem illogical or unreasonable. We feel that our emotional approach is accurate because we *feel* it; we feel that we are experiencing our emotions properly and thoroughly. So we begin to take pride in our emotions, and finally we begin to find ourselves so righteous that it is upsetting. We are extraordinarily passionate, proud, jealous, and justified because we have worked out our logic completely. But that process is problematic. At the beginner's level, we experience pure emotion; but then we dilute it; we try to control it. In the end, we find ourselves swimming in a pool of sewage, which is extraordinarily irritating, to say the least, and somewhat hellish, in fact.

The *Vajramala*, a text on kriya yoga, talks a great deal about working with the emotions. According to the *Vajramala* and its commentaries, kriya yoga separates emotions into two types: pure and impure. Pure emotion, which is the original flash of instantaneous experience, could be called wisdom, which is *jnana* in Sanskrit or *yeshe (ye-shes)* in Tibetan. With that first flash, we experience emotions properly and thoroughly, without preconceptions. At that level, emotion is insight. Then, as our emotions begin to deteriorate, as we begin to dilute them, they become ordinary passion, ordinary aggression, and ordinary ignorance. At that point they are regarded as dirt or impurity.

There is a definite division of experience into black and white in kriya yoga. The first impulse is regarded as purity, the true experience of reality in its fullest sense. Then we begin to water it down and mask that experience with all kinds of interpretations in an attempt to possess it. In doing so, the emotion becomes a confused one. So there is direct experience and there is a neurotic overlay, both happening at once. That original purity is vajra nature, which is inherently pure and cannot be contaminated—it cannot be destroyed *at all*. It is fundamental toughness. The moon might be behind a cloud, but the moon in itself is still pure. The cloud is the problem— if we sweep away the cloud the moon is sure to be a good moon.

One should see the neuroses clearly, look at them and study them, and finally flush them down the toilet. The way to do that is through various purification ceremonies and visualization practices. Purification in kriya yoga is a very personal experience, but solving our neurotic problems is not the point at all. Purification is learning to relate with the problems. Does a problem exist or not? Is the problem a problem, or is the problem a promise? We are not talking about how to get rid of problems or impurities here, as though we were suddenly surrounded by piles of garbage that we want to clean up. That is not the point. The point is to discover the quality of garbageness. Before we dispose of our garbage, first we have to examine it. If we approached purification as simply trying to get rid of our garbage, we would do a great job of emitting spiritual pollution into the atmosphere.

Having related with our garbage, the question of how we can purify ourselves is a question of surrendering. But all kinds of tricks are possible in this approach as well. We might say, "If I accept the whole thing and regard it as no big deal, then will I be free of any problems?" Those little tricks of ego, overlapping tricks of all kinds, go on constantly. The idea is to surrender completely.

The visualizations of kriya yoga are highly developed. They are very transparent visualizations, rather than simply imagining that we are a great guy or thinking of ourselves as a good person. In kriya yoga, visualization is identifying with our inherently pure psychological state of being, the part of us that is inherently innocent. The deities are visualized in the name of our innocence—or through the experience of our innocence. That innocent quality or pure aspect of our being is seen as a deity, as the embodiment of living enlightenment.

So kriya yoga's approach to life is segregation: certain parts of our life are good and pure, and certain parts of our life and our experience are impure, that is, diluted and contaminated by egocentricity. In kriya yoga we take the attitude that we are going to experience things very clearly and properly. We are not purely trying to relate with some abstract divinity or deity, but we are willing to relate with real experience.

CHAPTER FOURTEEN

Anuttara Yoga

The first three tantric yanas, kriyayoga yana, upayoga yana, and yoga yana, are called "lower tantra." And the last three tantric yanas, mahayoga yana, anuyoga yana, and atiyoga yana, are called "higher tantra." Anuttara yoga brings together the teachings of the lower tantra. It is usually not regarded as a separate yana but as the culmination of the first three. In some ways it acts as a bridge between the lower tantra and the higher tantra. The word *anuttara* (in Tibetan, *lame; bla-med*) literally means "nothing higher." As far as the lower tantras are concerned, anuttara is the highest tantric achievement. Many tantric practices, such as Kalacakra, Cakrasamvara, and Guhyasamaja, are based on anuttara yoga.

Earlier we discussed the principles of body, speech, and mind. It is through body, speech, and mind that we relate with the phenomenal world. Such a relationship is not necessarily spiritual; it is physical, bodily. It is a question of being a person of sanity, a person of openness. In fact, we could almost approach the whole path in a secular way and call it the nontheistic discipline of developing sanity and openness, rather than regarding it as purely a religious tradition.

In anuttara yoga, there is particular emphasis on speech. Speech is not only voice or verbal description, but any speechlike experience that brings a sense of rhythm or movement. In other words, it is energy or circulation rather than sound alone. We are not using speech here in the narrow sense, but we are speaking of speechlike situations, any interchange that exists, related with hearing, seeing, smelling, and the general sensory system of the body. As the basic communication that takes place in human society, speech is not limited to newspapers, television, and radio shows. More basically, it is a link between us and our body, a link between us and our mind. As such, speech brings mind to the cognitive level and body to the energetic level. Such a link, either with the mind or with the body, takes place constantly. That kind of movement and energy is speech.

Some kind of interchange takes place in our life constantly, which is known as energy. We are not talking about energy as a gigantic "voom!" that suddenly zaps us and makes us feel electrified. That kind of expectation seems to be a spiritual version of playing cowboys and Indians. When a local bandit swings open the bar door and walks in, suddenly tension builds up—there is obviously the possibility of a gunfight. We are not talking about energy at that level, even spiritually. Energy here is the self-existing energy that exists in every one of us. It is not particularly a sensation of electrified vibrations of energy. Such a sensation is very rare, if it happens at all. It could happen when we are at the height of our temper, but that is just one of those things that we do when we feel weak. When we don't feel so good, we might lose our temper to try to recharge ourselves. But energy is not necessarily so pathetic. Rather there is self-existing energy that goes on constantly, purely at the survival level. We exist, others exist, and therefore energy takes place constantly. There is energy of aggression, energy of passion, energy of depression, energy of excitement, energy of uncertainty, and so on.

According to the tantric tradition, beginning with upa yoga, yoga yana, and anuttara yoga, such energy is divided into three parts. The anuttara yoga model that we are going to discuss is based on *Kalacakra Tantra*. *Kala* means "time" and *cakra* is "wheel." So *Kalacakra* means "the wheel of time." *Tantra* in this context is used to designate a root text of vajrayana teachings. This tantra, as well as many others, describes three types of energy: *nadi, prana,* and *bindu.*

Nadi is like a channel. Energy has to have a channel, a way to journey, its own specialized path. Nadi is like a railroad track in that it provides a certain path or pattern that our energy follows. In this case, the phenomenal world has already created the sense of pattern for us. At this point the phenomenal world is not regarded as particularly radical or extraordinary. Rather, the phenomenal world has set up the system for us, so we personally do not have to set it up; the system is already there. We can build railroad cars with wheels, but the railroad tracks already exist. Taranatha, one of the Kalacakra tantric masters, likened the existence of nadi to putting boiled milk out in the cold air: the milk is sure to form its own skin. Boiling-hot milk has learned how to deal with reality by forming a skin. That is the railroad track that exists already. We don't have to try to find a transcendental world, a better world, or a world suited to tantra at all. This world exists as what we experience already, which is the notion of nadi.

The metaphor for prana is a horse looking for a rider. Such a horse has to be a good horse, well fed and strong. We are not using the horse as a metaphor for speed, but we are talking in terms of conviction, strength. Again, we are willing to relate with the existing world that has been set up for us. There is a highway already built for us, a supermarket built for us, shopping centers already built for us—there is already some kind of energy and pattern. So prana is the horse that rides on that energy, that rides on the existing tracks of the world, the nadi, that have already been set up.

Then there is bindu, the rider of the horse of prana. Bindu is a particular type of consciousness. The inquisitive quality of mind that tries to explore or to set up the universe is called *sem* (*sems*) in Tibetan. The definition of sem at this point is that which responds to reference points. Such a mind is willing to survey, willing to look into areas of energy. But sem purely responds to reference points, while bindu is the quality of mind that relates with the sense of journey. When we ride a horse, the horse just walks for us. We can't quite say the horse takes the journey; it just moves. The rider takes the journey, in that the rider controls the horse. It is the rider who looks right and left, ahead and behind, and appreciates the sights. This rider is bindu, which we could simply call consciousness.

So consciousness or bindu is journeying through the energies of the world. Consciousness is the awake quality that doesn't have to refer to immediate reference points alone, but has greater scope, like a radar system. Such a radar system has to be mounted in some kind of mechanical framework, which in this case is functional mind, sem. And that mounting has to be connected to the track by a wheel, which is prana. In other words, we have a radar system on a mounting that has a wheel that goes along a railway track. The radar system is called bindu, its mounting is sem, the wheel is prana, and the rail is nadi. In this case, it is bindu, the radar system, that guides or controls the journey. And the whole process is based on energy, obviously.

The tantric practices that work with nadi, prana, and bindu are based on hatha yoga, pranayama practices, and certain concentration and visualization experiences. But there is something more than that. In the application of nadi, prana, and bindu, there is still a sense of taking a journey, cranking up our machine along our railroad track. We can perceive our world in terms of nadi, prana, and bindu, and using them, we can take our journey. But then, at the highest level of anuttara yoga, we begin to transcend that journey; we go beyond using those three types of energy. We go on to something more than that, something beyond consciousness and mind, and our experience of the world alone. We begin to expand ourselves, and a greater openness begins to take place. It is like the unfolding of a flower: we don't even feel a sense of journey anymore. In anuttara yoga, that greater openness is symbolized by the monogram *evam*.

Discovering the existence of evam transcends hatha yoga and pranayama experience. *E* is the level of basic accommodation in which the attainment of buddhahood and the state of sentient beings are no longer different. At this point, naming somebody as a buddha or naming somebody as a sentient being is saying the same thing. When we say somebody is a buddha, that automatically is saying that he or she is no-buddha. In that sense, even the Buddha is no-buddha as well. A buddha exists only by the grace of somebody being no-buddha, or the reference point of somebody who is no-buddha. So sorting out buddhas and confused persons at this point is irrelevant. That is *e*. When you say *e*, it comes from your heart. You just breathe out—*ehhh*. It is a sound of opening up, without any particular definition or definite reference point. So *e* symbolizes the nonexistence of buddha and the nonexistence of sentient beings as either confused or enlightened beings.

Having that enormous space of *e* already, then you have *vam*. *Vam* is called the seed or the vajra-holder principle. Basically, *vam* is the son and *e* is the mother. When you have a mother, you have a son. That might mean that the son and the mother are separate, that they conflict with each other. However, the *vam* principle is that energy exists within the *e* of nonduality. Within the *e* of nonsamsara and nonnirvana, there is still basic energy.

Real energy exists as a sense of having a certain discipline, a certain experience, and a certain openness. If you had too much *e* you would space out and you wouldn't find anything anywhere; you wouldn't have any discipline. So evam brings the discipline of *vam* together with the spaciousness of *e*. Altogether, having transcended the three disciplines of nadi, prana, and bindu, you have a sense of openness or *e*, and then you have a sense of one-pointedness with concentrated energy or *vam*. The combination of *e* and *vam* brings together openness or spaciousness with indestructibility and one-pointedness. Evam is a central monogram or basic symbol of *Kalacakra Tantra*.

One of the basic points of anuttara tantra is that we are able to use any form of confusion or hallucination that we experience in ordinary everyday life. Actually, echo may be a better word than hallucination. First there is an experience and then there is the echo, the doubt or questioning: "Did I or didn't I?" Anuttara yoga brings out the constant doubt that goes on in the mind: "Am I or am I not? Did I experience that or didn't I experience that? Maybe something is just about to happen to me, maybe not." Such chatterings of mind take place all the time, but they are never legitimized in the Buddhist teachings of the hinayana and mahayana.

In the lower yanas, such questions are ignored. Such tentative explorations are ignored: "If you have any questions, regard them as your mind. Just say it's your mind; you're just confused. Just come back to your practice." But *Kalacakra Tantra* says such confusion is legitimate. In fact, such confusion has enormous potential. We have the potential of becoming an enormously successful—if we could use such a word—tantric student because we have such creepy questions about ourselves. Such double thinking, double hearing and double vision are legitimate. They are already included. When we experience this double vision, the first vision is sharp and then there is a shadow around that. The first vision is *vam*, and the second vision is *e*. That is exactly the process of evam: we have a sharp vision first and then we have a shadow around it. So we are seeing evam constantly. That is the basic approach of anuttara: allowing doubt, and including that doubt as part of our progress.

CHAPTER FIFTEEN

Maha Ati

The ninth yana, maha ati or ati yoga, is the final stage of the path. It is both the beginning and the end of the journey. It is not final in the sense that we have finished making a statement and we have nothing more to say, but final in the sense that we feel we have said enough. At this level, if there are any further words, they are the creations of space rather than idle remarks.

The tantric journey is like walking along a winding mountain path. Dangers, obstacles, and problems occur constantly. There are wild animals, earthquakes, landslides, all kinds of things, but still we continue on our journey and we are able to go beyond the obstacles. When we finally get to the summit of the mountain, we do not celebrate our victory. Instead of planting our national flag on the summit of the mountain, we look down again and see a vast perspective of mountains, rivers, meadows, woods, jungles, and plains. Once we are on the summit of the mountain, we begin to look down, and we feel attracted towards the panoramic quality of what we see. That is ati style. From that point of view, our achievement is not regarded as final but as a re-appreciation of what we have already gone through. In fact, we would like to retake the journey we have been through. So maha ati is the beginning of the end and the end of the beginning.

Ati teachings talk of enormous space. In this case, it is not space as opposed to a boundary, but a sense of total openness. Such openness can never be questioned. Ati yana is regarded as the king of all the yanas. In fact, the traditional Tibetan term for this yana, *long gyur thap kyi thekpa* (*klong gyur thabs kyi theg-pa*), means "imperial yana." It is imperial rather than regal, for while a king has conquered his own country, in order to be an emperor he has to conquer a lot of other territories and other continents as well. An emperor has no need for further conquests; his rule is beyond conquering. Likewise, ati is regarded as "imperial" because, from the perspective of ati yoga, hinayana discipline is seen as spaciousness; mahayana discipline is seen as spaciousness; and the tantric yanas, as well, are seen as spaciousness. If you review what we have been discussing throughout this book, you will see that we have been taking that point of view. We have discussed everything from the perspective of ati. Because of that, we have been able to view the characteristics of the various yanas and tantric disciplines in terms of openness and spaciousness and inevitability. That notion of wakefulness we have been discussing constantly is the final wakefulness of ati yoga.

Ati yoga teaching or discipline is sometimes defined as that which transcends coming, that which transcends going, and that which transcends dwelling. This definition is something more than the traditional tantric slogan of *advaita*, or "not two." In this case, we are looking at things from the level of true reality, not from the point of view of slogan or belief. Things are as they are, very simply, extremely simply so. Therefore things are unchanging, and therefore things are open as well. The relationship between us and our world is no relationship, because such a relationship is either there or not. We cannot manufacture a concept or idea of relationship to make us feel better.

From the perspective of ati, the rest of the yanas are trying to comfort us: "If you feel separate, don't worry. There is nonduality as your saving grace. Try to rest your mind in it. Everything is going to be okay. Don't cry." In contrast, the approach of ati is a blunt and vast attitude of total flop, as if the sky had turned into a gigantic pancake and suddenly descended onto our head, which ironically creates enormous space. That is the ati approach, that larger way of thinking, that larger view.

Buddhism has a number of schools, primarily divided into the hinayana, mahayana, and vajrayana traditions, and squabbling goes on among all of them. They all speak the language of totality, and every one of them claims to have the answer. The hinayanists may say that they have the answer because they know reality. The mahayanists may say that the bodhisattva is the best person that we could ever find in the world. Tantric practitioners may say that the most fantastic person is the powerful and crazy yogi who is unconquerable and who has achieved siddhis and magical powers of all kinds. Let them believe what they want. It's okay. But what do those things mean to us personally, as students who want to practice and who want to experience the teachings?

The maha ati practitioner sees a completely naked world, at the level of marrow, rather than skin or flesh or even bones. In the lower yanas, we develop lots of idioms and terms, and that makes us feel better because we have a lot of things to talk about, such as compassion or emptiness or wisdom. But in fact, that becomes a way of avoiding the actual naked reality of life. Of course, in maha ati there is warmth, there is openness, there is penetration—all those things are there. But if we begin to divide the dharma, cutting it into little pieces as we would cut a side of beef into sirloin steaks, hamburger, and chuck, with certain cuts of beef more expensive than others, then the dharma is being marketed. In fact, according to Vimalamitra, the reason maha ati is necessary is because throughout the eight lower yanas the dharma has been marketed as a particularly juicy morsel of food. The maha ati level is necessary in order to save the dharma from being parcelled and marketed; that is, it is necessary to preserve the wholesomeness of the whole path.

Actually, if we could make an ati yoga remark, all the yanas are purely creating successively more advanced and mechanized toys. At first, when a child is very young, we give him mobiles to look at, rings to suck, and rattles to shake. Then, when the child is more sophisticated, we give him more sophisticated toys, "creative play-things," and brightly colored bricks and sticks to put together. We provide even more sophisticated toys as the child becomes more and more inquisitive and sophisticated, and his mind and body are better coordinated.

Finally, at the level of adulthood, we continue to buy toys for ourselves. When we are old enough, we may buy ourselves a set of *Encyclopaedia Britannica*, or a stereo kit that we can put together. We may even build ourselves a house—the ultimate creative play-thing. Or we may invent some new gadget: "I designed a new kind of motor car, a new kind of airplane, a new kind of submarine. I built it and it actually worked. Isn't that fantastic?" We feel that our abilities are becoming much greater because not only can we build fantastic toys and enjoy them ourselves but we learn how to sell them, market them. When we become really sophisticated, we might design a zoo or even an entire city, and be accepted as important people in our society. It feels fantastic, extremely power-ful and encouraging. But we are still fascinated by our toys.

According to ati yoga, going through the yanas is similar to that process of collecting more and more toys. The more sophisticated and fascinated we become, the more we are actually reducing our-selves to a childlike level. Somehow we are not yet at the level of maha ati if we are still fascinated by our toys, our occupations, no matter how extensive or expansive they may be. At the maha ati level, those little tricks that we play to improve ourselves or to entertain ourselves are no longer regarded as anything—but at the same time they are everything, much vaster than we could have imagined. It is as though we were building a city or a zoo, and suddenly the whole sky turned into a gigantic pancake and dropped on us. There is a new dimension of surprise that we never thought of, we never expected. We never expected the sky to drop on our head.

There is a children's story about the sky falling, but we do not actually believe that such a thing could happen. The sky turns into a blue pancake and drops on our head—nobody believes that. But in maha ati experience, it actually does happen. There is a new dimen-sion of shock, a new dimension of logic. It is as though we were furiously calculating a mathematical problem in our notebook, and suddenly a new approach altogether dawned on us, stopping us in our tracks. Our perspective becomes completely different.

Our ordinary approach to reality and truth is so poverty stricken that we don't realize that the truth is not one truth, but all truth. It could be everywhere, like raindrops, as opposed to water coming out of a faucet that only one person can drink from at a time. Our limited approach is a problem. It may be our cultural training to believe that only one person can get the truth: "You can receive this, but nobody else can." There are all sorts of philosophical, psychological, religious, and emotional tactics that we use to motivate ourselves, which say that we can do something but nobody else can. Since we think we are the only one that can do something, we crank up our machine and we do it. And if it turns out that somebody else has done it already, we begin to feel jealous and resentful. In fact, the dharma has been marketed or auctioned in that way. But from the point of view of ati, there is "all" dharma rather than "the" dharma. The notion of "one and only" does not apply anymore. If the gigantic pancake falls on our head, it falls on everybody's head.

In some sense it is both a big joke and a big message. You cannot even run to your next-door neighbor saying, "I had a little pancake fall on my head. What can I do? I want to wash my hair." You have nowhere to go. It is a cosmic pancake that falls everywhere on the face of the earth. You cannot escape—that is the basic point. From that point of view, both the problem and the promise are cosmic.

If you are trying to catch what I am saying, quite possibly you cannot capture the idea. In fact, it is quite possible that you do not understand a word of it. You cannot imagine it in even the slightest, faintest way. But it is possible that there are situations that exist beyond your logic, beyond your system of thinking. That is not an impossibility. In fact it is highly possible.

The earlier yanas talk about the rug being pulled out from under our feet, which is quite understandable. If our landlord kicks us out of our apartment, the rug is pulled out from under our feet, obviously. That is quite workable, and we find that we can still relate with our world. But in ati we are talking about the sky collapsing onto us. *Nobody* thinks of that possibility. It is an entirely different approach. No one can imagine a landlady or a landlord who could pull that trick on us.

In maha ati we are not talking about gaining ground or losing ground, or how we settle down and find our way around. Instead we are talking about how we can develop headroom. Headroom, or the space above us, is the important thing. We are interested in how space could provide us with a relationship to reality, to the world.

I do not think we should go into too much detail about maha ati. I have basically been finger painting, but that is as far as we can go at this point. However, we could discuss another topic that is closely related to ati yana: crazy wisdom.

Using the word *crazy* from the English language to describe tantric experience is very tricky because of the various ideas we have about craziness. In the American Indian tradition there was a warrior named Crazy Horse. He was a crazy, old, wise eccentric, who was a great warrior and had tremendous courage. Being crazy is also associated with the idea of being absurd, on the verge of lunacy. There is also a notion of craziness as being unconventional. And sometimes we talk about somebody being crazy about music or crazy about honey or sugar. We mean that somebody takes excessive pleasure in something or has an excessive fascination, to the point where he might destroy himself by being so crazy about whatever it is.

We might also say that someone is crazy if he doesn't agree with us. For instance, if we are trying to form a business, we will approach somebody to be our business partner who agrees with our business proposals. We tell him that the two of us can make lots of money. And if we approach this "uncrazy" person properly, he will accept our logic and he will love the idea of going into business with us. Whereas if we approach an intelligent "crazy" person, he will see through us. He will see any holes in our plan or any neurosis that our business might create. So we don't want to approach such a person as a business partner: "I won't talk to him. He's crazy." What we mean is, "He will see through me. He won't buy my simplistic

logic, my trip." That description of craziness comes somewhat close
to the tantric idea of craziness. Still, such craziness has a sense of
basic ground. There is a lot of room, a lot of trust, but there is also a
lot of solidity.

We might also view our grandparents' orthodoxy as crazy. They
are so soaked in their own culture and their own norms that they
don't understand our culture at all. Their crazy ways make them
practically unapproachable to us. We cannot shake their faith and
their convictions, and we feel frustrated when we have something to
say to them and they don't respond as we want. So we might regard
them as semi-crazy.

I don't think crazy wisdom fits any of the examples above.
Instead crazy wisdom is the basic norm or the basic logic of sanity. It
is a transparent view that cuts through conventional norms or conventional emotionalism. It is the notion of relating properly with the
world. It is knowing how much heat is needed to boil water to make
a cup of tea, or how much pressure you should apply to educate
your students. That level of craziness is very wise. It is based on
being absolutely wise, knowing exactly what to do. Such a wise
person is well versed in the ways of the world, and he has developed
and understood basic logic. He knows how to build a campfire, how
to pitch a tent, and how to brush his teeth. He knows how to handle
himself in relating with the world, from the level of knowing how to
make a good fire in the fireplace up to knowing the fine points of
philosophy. So there is absolute knowledgeability. And then, on top
of that, craziness begins to descend, as an ornament to the basic
wisdom that is already there.

In other words, crazy wisdom does not occur unless there is a
basic understanding of things, a knowledge of how things function as
they are. There has to be trust in the normal functioning of karmic
cause and effect. Having been highly and completely trained, then
there is enormous room for crazy wisdom. According to that logic,
wisdom does not exactly go crazy; but on top of the basic logic or
basic norm, craziness as higher sanity, higher power, or higher
magic, can exist.

One attribute of crazy wisdom is fearlessness. Having already
understood the logic of how things work, fearlessness is the further

power and energy to do what needs to be done, to destroy what needs to be destroyed, to nurse what should be nursed, to encourage what should be encouraged, or whatever the appropriate action is.

The fearlessness of crazy wisdom is also connected with bluntness. Bluntness here is the notion of openness. It is a sense of improvising, being resourceful, but not in the sense of constantly trying to improvise the nature of the world. There are two approaches to improvising. If we have a convenient accident and we capitalize on that, we improvise as we go along. That is the conventional sense of the word. For instance, we might become a famous comedian, not because of our perceptiveness, but purely because we make funny mistakes. We say the wrong things at the wrong time and people find us hilarious. Therefore we become a famous comedian. That is approaching things from the back door, or more accurately, it is like hanging out in the backyard.

The other approach to improvising, or bluntness, is seeing things as they are. We might see humor in things; we might see strength or weakness. In any case, we see what is there quite bluntly. A crazy wisdom person has this sense of improvising. If such a person sees that something needs to be destroyed rather than preserved, he strikes on the spot. Or if something needs to be preserved, although it might be decaying or becoming old hat, he will nurse it very gently.

So crazy wisdom is absolute perceptiveness, with fearlessness and bluntness. Fundamentally, it is being wise, but not holding to particular doctrines or disciplines or formats. There aren't any books to follow. Rather, there is endless spontaneity taking place. There is room for being blunt, room for being open. That openness is created by the environment itself. In fact, at the level of crazy wisdom, all activity is created by the environment. The crazy wisdom person is just an activator, just one of the conditions that have evolved in the environment.

Since we are reaching the end of our tantric journey together, so to speak, I would like to say something about how you could relate to all of this information that you have received. You don't have to try to catch the universe in the same way that you would try to catch a grasshopper or a flea. You don't *have* to do something with what you have experienced, particularly. Why don't you let it be as it is? In fact, that might be necessary. If you actually want to use something, you have to let it be. You cannot drink all the water on earth in order to quench your thirst eternally. You might drink a glass of water, but you have to leave the rest of the water, rivers, and oceans so that if you are thirsty again, you can drink more. You have to leave some room somewhere. You don't have to gulp everything down. It's much nicer not to do that; in fact, it is polite.

If you are terribly hungry and thirsty, you want to attack the universe as your prey all at once: "I'll have it for my dinner or my breakfast. I don't care." You don't think about anybody else who might have just a humble request, who might just want to have a sip from your glass of milk or a piece of meat from your plate. If you are told that you should be devotional, you might think that means that you should be even more hungry and try to get every possible blessing into your system. Since you are hungry, you suck up everything, all the systems and resources that exist, including your own. You don't find yourself being a productive human being; instead you find yourself becoming a monster.

There are a lot of problems with that, unless you have the umbrella notion of maha ati, which says: "It's okay. Everything is okay. Just take a pinch of salt, a spoonful of soy sauce. Just take one shot of whiskey. Don't rush; everything is going to be okay. You can have plenty of room if you want. Just cool it." You don't have to do a complete job, all at once. If you go too far, if you are too hungry, you could become a cosmic monster. That message is very courageous, but very few people have the courage to say that.

I am actually concerned and somewhat worried about how you are going to handle all this material. You could overextend yourselves and get completely zonked or completely bewildered. Or you could use this as just another clever reference point, a new vocabulary or logic to manipulate your friends and your world. What you do with this material is really up to you. I hope that you will feel grateful for this introduction to the tantric world, and I hope that you will

142 JOURNEY WITHOUT GOAL

realize from this that the world is not all that bad and confused. The world can be explored; it is workable, wherever you go, whatever you do. But I would like to plant one basic seed in your mind: I feel that it is absolutely important to make the practice of meditation your source of strength, your source of basic intelligence. Please think about that. You could sit down and do nothing, just sit and do nothing. Stop acting, stop speeding. Sit and do nothing. You should take pride in the fact that you have learned a very valuable message: you actually can survive beautifully by doing nothing.

Lord Marpa's Praise
to the Gurus

Lord Akṣobhya, Mahāsukhakāya,
United with Vajraḍākinī,
Chief of ḍākas,
Śrī Heruka, I praise you and prostrate.

Collector of commands and secret mantras,
Possessor of the Secret,
Propagator of the holy dharma in the world of men,
Lord Nāgārjuna, father and son, I praise you.

You who bring down the overwhelming vajra thunderbolt,
The kind one who protects from fear,
Tilopa, lord of the three levels,
Who has attained supreme siddhi, I praise you.

Undergoing twelve trials attending the guru,
All the piṭakas and tantras
You realized in an instant;
Lord Buddha in human form, I praise you.

Indestructible form of mahāmudrā,
Possessing the uncontrived primordial essence,

Realizing the truth of the bliss of simplicity,
Lord Prince Maitrīpa, I praise at your feet.

Expounding the doctrine of the command lineage,
Attaining the siddhi of the profound Guhyasamāja,
You are endowed with compassion and wisdom,
Jñānagarbha, I praise at your feet.

Dwelling in charnel grounds, solitudes, and under trees,
A kusulu savoring potency,
Possessing the miracle of traveling in space,
Kukkurīpā, I praise you.

Having realized the truth of abundance,
Possessing the potency of moonbeams,
You satisfy and bring bliss to those who see you,
Yoginī, I praise you.

Resting in the shade of the excellent umbrella
Adorned with golden ribbons,
Seated in the sky, attaining mastery over the sun and moon
Jetsüns of Nepal, I praise you.

Overcoming the worldly attachment of grasping and fixation,
Possessing the benefit of attending the guru,
Holding principally to the practice of enlightenment,
Preserving the learning of mahāyāna,
Clearing away obstructions as well as obstacles caused by agents of
    perversion,
The friend who introduces one to the good guru,
Guiding masters, I praise you.

The merit of praising the guru
Is equal to offering to the buddhas of the three times.
By this merit of praising the masters,
May all beings attend spiritual friends.

Translated by the Nālandā Translation Committee.

Index

Chögyam Trungpa, Rinpoche, is the former abbot of the Surmang monasteries and a meditation master of the Kagyü and Nyingma lineages of Tibetan Buddhism. He holds the degree of Khenpo, the equivalent of a Doctor of Divinity degree in the West and has also studied at Oxford University as a Spaulding Fellow. He is the author of many books on Buddhism and the path of meditation, among them *Meditation in Action*, *Cutting Through Spiritual Materialism*, and *The Myth of Freedom*.

Trungpa Rinpoche was invited to the United States in 1970 and shortly thereafter founded Vajradhatu. Vajradhatu is comprised of more than sixty-five meditation and study centers located in major cities in the United States, Canada, and Europe. The centers offer programs in the study of Buddhist philosophy and psychology and the practice of meditation. Two rural centers, Karmê-Chöling in Vermont and Rocky Mountain Dharma Center in northern Colorado, provide the opportunity to study and practice in a more contemplative environment.

In 1974 Trungpa Rinpoche established Nalanda Foundation, a nonsectarian educational organization; its divisions include Shambhala Training, a secular meditation program, and Naropa Institute, an innovative liberal arts college.

Information on any of the Vajradhatu centers can be obtained by writing to Vajradhatu, 1345 Spruce Street, Boulder, Colorado 80302. For information about programs offered by Naropa Institute, please write to the Institute at 1111 Pearl Street, Boulder, Colorado 80302. A catalogue of cassette recordings and transcripts of lectures by Trungpa Rinpoche is available from the Naropa Institute Bookstore, 2011 10th Street, Boulder, Colorado 80302.